This Book Belongs To...

....

....

....

....

Color By Number Coloring Book For Kids Ages 8-12

This coloring book features:

- 50 unique stress-relieving color by number designs.
- Each page is printed on a single side making them easy to remove for display
- Each page is professionally composed to provide the highest quality
- Perfect for anyone who enjoys art.
- Each page is 8.5 inches by 11 inches
- Printed on bright white paper, 60-pound stock
- Order your copy today

Makes a wonderful and unique gift!
Get Your Copy Today!

Color Test Pages

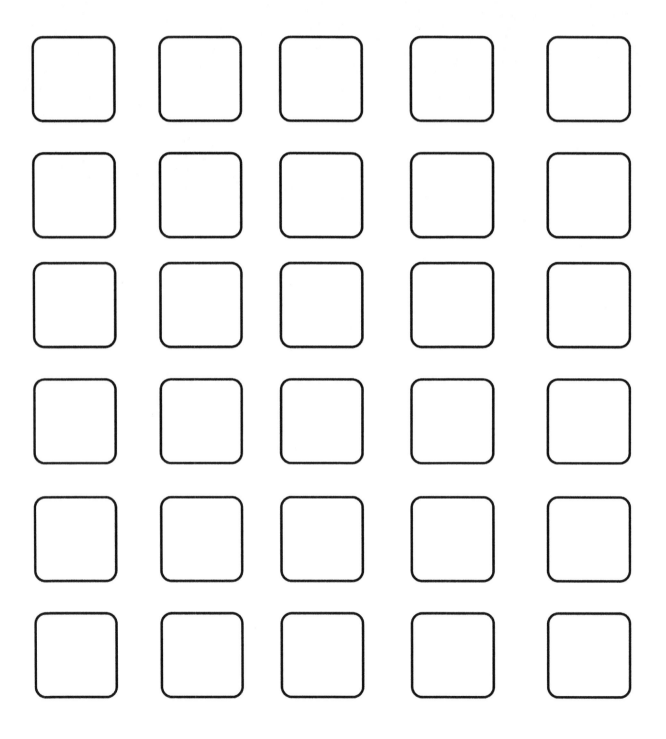

1-WHITE 2-RED 3-GREEN 4-ORANGE 5-GRAY 6-YELLOW

1-PINK 2-BROWN 3-GREEN 4-LIGHT BROWN 5-LIGHT GREEN

1-WHITE 2-RED 3- GREEN 4-YELLOW 5-PINK 6-ORANGE 7-DARK GREEN

1-LAVENDER 2-ROSE 3-RED 4-PURPLE 5-GREEN 6-YELLOW 7-PURPLE 8-LAVENDER

1- GREEN 2- PINK 3- RED 4- FIR GREEN 5- WHITE 6- YELLOW 7- LAUREL

1-WHITE 2-BLUE 3-YELLOW 4-RED 5-GREEN 6-ORANGE 7-DARK GREEN

1-ORANGE 2-RED 3-YELLOW 4- PINK 5-BROWN 6-GREEN

1-WHITE 2-RED 3-GREEN 4-YELLOW 5-PINK

1-WHITE 2-LIGHT YELLOW 3-GREEN 4-BEIGE 5-BROWN 6-PINK

1-WHITE 2-RED 3-GREEN 4-PEACH 5-YELLOW 6-PINK

1-WHITE 2-RED 3-GREEN 4-ORANGE 5-BROWN 6-PEACH 7-PINK

1-WHITE 2-RED 3-GREEN 4-ORANGE 5-YELLOW 6-PINK 7-PEACH

1-ORANGE 2-RED 3-GREEN 4-YELLOW 5-SILVER 6-PINE GREEN

1-ORANGE 2-RED 3-WHITE 4-BLUE 5-YELLOW 6-GREEN 7-BROWN

1 PINK 2-RED 3-BROWN 4-GREEN 5-YELLOW

1 PINK 2-RED 3-PEACH 4- GREEN 5-BROWN 6-YELLOW

1-BEIGE 2-BROWN 3-ROSE 4-ORANGE 5-RED 6-YELLOW 7-GREEN

1-WHITE 2-RED 3-YELLOW 4-ORANGE 5-GREEN 6-PINK 7-PEACH

1 LIGHT GREEN 2 RED 3 PINK 4 YELLOW 5 GREEN

1-WHITE 2-BROWN 3-YELLOW 4-RED 5-GREEN 6-PINK 7-GRAY

1-WHITE 2-RED 3-GREEN 4-YELLOW 5-BROWN 6-PINK

1-BLANC 2-ROUGE 3-VERTS 4-JAUNES 5-BRUNS 6-ORANGES 7-ROSES

1-WHITE 2-RED 3-GREEN 4-ORANGE 5-PINK 6-YELLOW 7-PEACH

1-Sky Blue 2-Green 3-Yellow 4-Red
5-Navy Green 6-Orange

1-Gray 2-Pink 3-Light yellow
4-Orange 5-Green 6-Sky Blue

1-yellow 2-Light Pink 3-Light blue
4-dark blue 5-Gold 6-Pink

1-Red 2-Indigo 3-Pink
4-Light Yellow 5-Brown 6-Blue

1-Pink 2-Black 3-Light Green
4-Green 5-Yellow 6-Brown

1-Light Yellow 2-Pink 3-Red
4-orange 5-Light Blue 6-Green

1-Indigo 2-Pink 3-Red
4-Blue 5-Green 6-Light Blue

1-Green 2-Yellow 3-Pink
4-Grey 5-Brown 6-Light Blue

1-Black 2-Light green 3-Light yellow
4-Orange 5-Dark 6-light Blue

1-Pink 2-Blue 3-indigo
4-Dark Yellow 5-Light Blue 6-Green

1-Bronze 2-Supernova 3-Carnation Pink
4-Dusty Gray 5-Atlantis 6-Japanese Laurel

1-Green Haze 2-Dodger Blue 3-Anakiwa

4-Heliotrope 5-Bright Sun 6-Crusta

1-Electric Violet 2-Scarlet 3-Vis Vis
4-Mine Shaft 5-Malachite 6-Anakiwa

1-Anakiwa 2-Dodger Blue 3-Tree Poppy
4-Broom 5-Malachite 6-Mauve

1-Green Haze 2-Anakiwa 3-Cream
4-Orange Peel 5-Mauve 6-Heliotrope

1-Yellow 2-Red 3-Orange 4-Green 5-Light Pink 6-Sky Blue

1-Light Pink 2-Gray 3-Yellow 4-Green 5-Blue 6-Sky Blue

1-Yellow 2-Pink 3-Red 4-Orange 5-Sky Blue 6-Green

1-Green 2-Yellow 3-Red
4-Indigo 5-Sky Blue 6-Pink

1-Yellow 2-Brown 3-Red 4-Orange 5-Sky Blue 6-Green

1-Anakiwa 2-Supernova 3-Dusty Gray
4-Pink Salmon 5-Atlantis 6-Japanese Laurel

1- Green 2- Black 3- Red 4- Brown
5- Light Blue 6- Blue

1-Green Haze 2-Mauve 3-Anakiwa
4-Flint 5-Vermilion 6-Heliotrope

1-Indigo 2-Dark Blue 3-Yellow
4-Red 5-Green 6-Light Blue

1-Carnation Pink 2-Golden Tainoi 3-Brown
4-Peach Orange 5-Onahau 6-Chartreuse

Printed in Great Britain
by Amazon

78956082R00059

The New Brand Ninja Foodi Cookbook for UK

Super Easy and Budget Friendly Recipes to Fry, Bake, Grill, and Roast with Your Ninja Foodi Pressure Cooker

Oliver M. Payne

Table of Contents

All you need to know about the Ninja Foodi Pressure Cooker

In the better part of this year, with all my outright curiosity in looking for a better gadget for cooking, I came across a beautiful pressure cooker that has since capitalized on my kitchen. The UK Foodi pressure cooker has actualized and improvised my cooking, reducing the tedious work I have always encountered in my kitchen, like rolling dough after a long day of work.

The appliance has enabled me to whip up impressive dinners even though I am not a professional chef. For instance, cooking a chuck roast, baking a cake, and lip-smacking French fries. Although my menu has not changed substantively, the Foodi pressure cooker has strengthened my kitchen goal of attaining crispy and tasty food with natural nutritional value.

Currently preparing crispy food using the multipurpose pan through its detachable diffuser and crisping basket with separate accessories has offered excellent functionality in my kitchen. I can now prepare diverse kinds of recipes that I could not make before through its functional capabilities.

Additionally, in the time I have used the Ninja foodi pressure cooker, I have made an exemplary pace in preparing roast potatoes, frying chips, and baking cakes that are super cool, improving my kitchen performance. My menu also has exceeded the expectation I had as I can now prepare amazing chili con carne, steaming vegetables, slow-cooked sausage stew, and pressure-cooked risotto.

In this cookbook, you will learn the basics of the Ninja pressure cooker, why I choose the pressure cooker, the benefits of using the pressure cooker, and the primary functions of the digital gadget that has entered the market. Furthermore, you will get valuable insights on the user guide of the Ninja Foodi pressure cooker, on the way to maintain and clean it, alongside essential tricks and tips to keep in mind when using this Ninja Foodi pressure cooker.

What is Ninja Foodi Pressure Cooker?

Ninja Foodie is an efficient pressure cooker and a great air fryer that can be used as a roaster, steamer, oven, slow cooker, and dehydrator. The pressure cooker crisps and steams food according to the user's needs; thus, it is all in one cooking pot. Essentially, the Foodi pressure cooker comes in handy in three cooking modes: crisp steam mode, air frying mode, and pressure mode.

The modes serve vital functions like cooking a whole chicken, fresh yogurt, and loaves of bread, among others, to bring the best convenience and functionality. Using the pressure cooker can allow the cooking of ingredients with a crispy texture, which ensures food is delicious and stands out from the crowd.

The pressure cooker can cook chicken nuggets and frozen French fries while monitoring the results for crispiness and even cooking. Moreover, homemade yogurt, batches of risotto, slow pulled chicken, and crusty bread are best cooked through a Foodi pressure cooker. Owning the pressure cooker untethers you from having three different and separate appliances: a slow cooker, an air fryer, and a pressure cooker.

This pressure cooker has a bulky lid that opens on a side hinge; thus, it cannot be fully tucked under the kitchen cupboard alongside its overall size. That makes the pressure cooker comfortably fit in your kitchen.

The settings of the cooker are digitally controlled via the front panel that is located below the digital display. When cooking, the time counts down on the screen, giving a clear glance on track of timings. With its diverse programmed settings, the machine is a perfect match with its unprecedented versatility and its quiet nature.

Why I choose the Ninja Pressure cooker

I choose the Ninja pressure cooker since it has fewer buttons than instant pots. Also, it has superb screens that can light up specific choices; thus, you cannot be tempted to pick the wrong mode with a different function.

In addition, the Ninja pressure cooker has the added ability to function like an air fryer meaning you can cook crispy and delicious meals free from excess calories and cholesterol through the pressure cooker.

For the time I have used the pressure cooker, I have enjoyed tasty meals that I cook efficiently within a short period. With a Ninja pressure cooker, I cannot worry about the small capacity compared to instant pots I have used before, as it has three cooking modes that enhance the cooking process to more than 70 percent.

Alternatively, the Ninja pressure cooker is a convenient pot with one hinged lid that performs every function, thus, enhancing the cooking process to be an entertaining journey. Buying and using the Ninja pressure cooker has offered me professional-grade results with large portioned healthier meals.

Ninja pressure cooker is easy to use since it does not skimp its effectiveness by overloading its function list. Also, the pressure parts are well labeled, with control panel features being readable to ease the customized settings and enhance the functionality of the buttons. All these features have streamlined how I organize the recipes I can make in a day.

Main functions of Ninja Foodi

With Ninja foodi pressure cooker, you can easily and quickly build delicious homemade snacks, meals, desserts, and sides. The exclusive pressure cooker utilizes tender crisp technology, which is prolific in making the food perfectly with a golden finish through its sleek, multifunctional, stylish design.

The Foodi pressure cooker also comes with accessories such as a basket for air frying, two racks, and a cookbook. So, the accessories make the appliance excellent for baking and air-frying foods. The Ninja Foodi serves the following 14 primary functions through the three switching modes that are highly developed:

- Air fry
- Pressure
- Broil
- Crisp and steam for making meals at once
- Roast and bake
- Dehydrate
- Steam and bake for baking quick bread and cakes
- Proof for helping the dough to rise evenly
- Keep warm
- Slow cook
- Sous vide for preparing food sealed in a plastic bag regulated by bath water.
- Yogurt for fermenting and pasteurizing milk into homemade yogurt.
- Sauté/sear to keep the pot like a stovetop
- Steam

The Foodi cooker operates through an intelligent cook system with additional accessories that are highly developed. You do not need to swap the pressure cooker because the lid serves every function. The impeccable nature of this cooker enhances even temperature distribution to cooking foods that match your preferential taste.

It is plastered with steel and plastic matte on the exterior to enhance exemplary performance through the highlight functions and adjusts timings for temperatures alongside start and stop buttons.

The stand-out functions of the Foodi Ninja pressure cooker are dehydrating alternatives, slow cooking, and air crisping. Also, with sauté and sear functions, you can prepare slow cooker beef stew by browning the meat, with the resulting dishes being moist and requiring a bit of thickening.

When using the Foodi pressure cooker, ensure you reduce the liquid quantities in recipes with all tender ingredients other than overcooked, as it retains its rich flavor. After the allocated time elapses, the cooker switches digitally to keep warm mode and starts reading up from zero. The ceramic coatings of the Ninja food ease the washing process manually because the slow cooker is not dishwasher safe.

Removing the silicone seal around the internal rim of the slow cooker ensures you get some splashes. Using the air crisp function offers a better way of cooking healthier food free from oil. For instance, when cooking French fries, you can shuffle them halfway, and this requires a lifting lid that automatically pauses the cooking. The dehydrator creates an intensifying flavor, dried apple, and tasty soft slices that leave the food crispy.

Benefits of using Ninja Foodi Pressure cooker

The Ninja pressure cooker has substantive benefits, from making fresh yogurt to excellent loaves of bread. Here is a look at the typical benefits of this magnificent cooker:

1. Cooks faster

Cooking using a pressure cooker is fourfold faster than the regular oven. For instance, the black bean usually takes approximately 2 hours and can only require 10 to 15 minutes in a Ninja pressure cooker. Also, a whole chicken needs only five per pound, unlike 15 minutes per pound when cooked in an oven, with Ninja pressure cooker cooking healthier foods even during busy nights.

2. Increases safety

A pressure cooker is a safer option than the top stove cooking method. If a boiling pot or frying pan, uncovered or covered, gets bumped when cooking, it can fall off or splash off the stove can, cause severe burns or scalding to anyone around. Since the pressure cooker has a safer secured lid on the pot, it cannot harm an individual even when the pot is bumped and falls off the stove as its contents remain inside.

3. Pressurizes and steams food

The pressure cooker pressurizes and steams food, making it ideal for boiling, baking, and pan-frying. The lid has a tight airlock for trapping heat inside, which results in pressure and steam surrounding the food evenly on all sides. These conditions make temperatures inside the pressure cooker hotter, unlike other cooking methods.

Even though water boils at 212F, pressure cooker temperature can reach 250F. Since water is an effective conductor of air, it raises the pressure cooker's temperature to higher than a conventional oven in the same environment.

4. Retains nutritional value and flavor in food

Sometimes food loses its fantastic flavor and nutritional value when cooked through diverse methods. Ninja pressure cooker achieves this by lowering cooking time, thus, avoiding overcooking the food. However, this is different from the Ninja pressure cooker, as it preserves nutrient value and flavor most efficiently.

The steam and pressure that builds up in a pressure cooker seal the moisture, thus enhancing the prolific natural flavors of foods. Since natural flavors are inbuilt and sealed, chefs cannot over-rely heavily on seasonings with high preservative content and heavy sodium.

Cooking using a Ninja pressure cooker holds more minerals and vitamins, unlike other cooking methods that boil it away. In addition, if you utilize an available cooking rack in a pressure cooker, most fats will get drained away.

5. Healthier cooking

Since the Ninja pressure cooker is developed with an air fryer, it enables healthier means of cooking as it saves on severe calorie levels by minimizing excess oils. The cooker is customized with easy-to-use features and buttons, and the multi-cooker truly saves on using cheaper ingredients for cooking in your modern kitchen. Essentially, you will achieve tasty and nutritious foods that are free from cholesterol which is essential in offering you a healthier lifestyle with any recipe you prepare.

User guide of Ninja Foodi Pressure cooker
How to clean and maintain

Keeping your Ninja Foodi clean without damaging it is easy. The Foodie pressure cooker comes in handy with two cooking lids for pressure cooking and air frying. The deep pot can sauce platter or oil all over the crisping lid easing the maintenance and cleaning process. Therefore, deep cleaning the pressure cooker is the best option you can embrace to ensure it does not smell or lose its practical functionality.

Here is a step-by-step process of keeping your Ninja Foodi pressure cooker well by deep cleaning:

1. Turn off then unplug the device to ensure your safety is guaranteed

Dismantle all removable parts by taking them out. The parts include trays, drip racks, pans, and all other accessories.

2. Clean removable parts using warm soapy water.

Do not use abrasive components to scrub the pressure cooker parts because putting any part in a dishwasher is unsafe, as you will have to wipe things down manually.

3. Put away caked-in food inside the basket or oven.

Move further and peer inside the foodi basket or oven; you may notice grease or clumpy food attached to the sides of the pressure cooker. After loosening the greasy parts with a toothpick, use a damp cloth to remove the residue, and do not scrub very hard because you will damage the Foodi.

4. Clean the lid of the air fryer separately.

Unscrew the lid of the pressure cooker using a screwdriver alongside warm soapy water like other components. Ensure all residues are removed after screwing on the lid back.

5. Wipe the exterior of the Ninja Foodie pressure cooker since it is greasy.

The procedure should be a regular habit since greasy coatings affect the working and state of the Foodi pressure cooker.

6. Put the components of the Foodi pressure cooker back in and let it dry before preparing another meal.

All components should be put together correctly to minimize the chances of dumbing, which can cause severe burns during the cooking process.

Note: It is wise to manually deep clean your Ninja pressure cooker since it is not dishwasher safe to achieve a pleasant smell. After cleaning the components of the pressure cooker, ensure you use a damp or microfiber cloth to wipe the lid and the grill. All these processes ensure your foodi pressure cooker works excellently and efficiently, giving you value for your money.

Tips and tricks

As a user, it is wise to learn the ideal essentials of the Ninja foodie pressure cooker to adeptly upraise your cooking procedure. Therefore, here is a look at essential basics you can apply when using every Ninja Foodi:

1. Avoid oven cleaners or harsh chemicals when using your Foodi pressure cooker.

Foods with chemicals can discolor and damage your pressure cooker. So warm water and soap are vital products you should take advantage of.

2. Ninja Foodi pressure cookers are not dishwasher safe

Most components of the Ninja pressure cooker can get damaged or warped when put in the dishwasher. Washing them manually is the best option as it involves a suitable handling procedure.

3. If you need deep cleaning, utilize a mixture of water and baking soda.

The paste helps scrub your food without damaging your food and making future snacks come into contact with chemicals.

4. Doing a basic clean wash after each use is essential

This is done by pressure cooking 1 cup of lemon juice and hot water in the food pressure cooker for about 10 minutes; afterward, wipe it gently with a paper towel.

5. Heat the pressure cooker right

Turn on the nob of the Ninja pressure cooker to start your cooking process right away. Avoid foods that take very long to heat up as they can be overcooked because you may make incorrect timings. Recipes may provide unreliable timings as cooking time may differ substantively from when the optimum pressure has been reached.

The Ninja pressure cookers are the best kitchen gadgets individuals keep embracing as it is easy to use. Though it is expensive, the pressure cooker multifunction's as it can work like an air fryer and pressure cooker. For the time I have used the Ninja pressure cooker, I can attest that my kitchen setting has been revolutionized.

Generally, Ninja foodi pressure cooker is a multipurpose, industrial-size appliance with excellent modes, and you do need to purchase a separate pressure cooker, air fryer, and slow cooker. All work together, with each feature working differently in serving a particular function.

Cumberland sausages with onion gravy

Prep time: 40 minutes
Cook time: 1 hour, 20 min

Serves 4Ingredients
- 8 Cumberland sausages (make sure they're gluten-free if you need them to be)
- Rapeseed oil for drizzling
- 2 small onions
- Mashed potatoes to serve (optional)

For the gravy
- 3 large onions, finely sliced
- 1 large red onion, finely sliced
- 1 tbsp light brown sugar
- 2 tbsp balsamic vinegar
- ½ bunch thyme leaves picked and a few sprigs reserved to garnish
- 3 bay leaves
- 1 tsp pink peppercorns lightly crushed
- 500ml beef stock
- 500ml chicken stock
- 1 tbsp redcurrant jelly or blackcurrant jam

Preparation Instructions

1. Over medium heat, add the butter and oil to the big pan to start making the gravy. Once the butter has melted, add all the sliced onions with a big pinch of salt. Stir until the onions are all coated in the fat and are gently sizzling, then add 1 tbsp water, cover, and turn the heat down to low. Stirring continuously, cook gently for 20 minutes.

2. Take off the lid, add the sugar and vinegar, then slightly increase the heat and continue cooking for another 20 minutes while stirring more frequently. It's okay for the onions to catch on the bottom a little, but you don't want to burn them; add a little water if necessary.

3. Stir gently to mix the pink peppercorns, bay leaves, and thyme before adding the meat and chicken stock. Make sure you scrape up any bits stuck to the bottom of the pan, as this does make all the difference. Bring to a boil, decrease the heat to a simmer, and cook for at least 45 minutes, or until the mixture has been slowly reduced down to a thick gravy.

4. Heat the oven to 160°C fan/gas 4 before starting to cook the sausages. Put the sausages in a baking dish, ensuring they're not too crowded, and drizzle with a little oil. After giving them a good toss to evenly distribute the coating, bake for 30 minutes, turning them over once.

5. Over medium-high heat, add a drizzle of oil to a large pan. Halve the 2 small onions (with the peel on) then put them cut-side down in the pan. Don't remove the cover while they steam in the pan for an additional 5 minutes after the heat is turned off. Cover them and cook for 8 minutes, or until the cut side has charred and the insides have softened.

6. Slip the peel off the onions, cut 1 of them into wedges, and carefully lower them into the gravy to lightly glaze and warm through while the sausages finish cooking. Add the jelly/jam and taste for seasoning. Serve the sausages with plenty of onions and gravy (you can strain the gravy if you like, but leaving in a few of the sticky onions tastes great too) with mashed potatoes on the side, if you like.

Nutritional values Per Serving

Calories: 706	fat: 42.2g
protein: 27.7g	carbs: 34.6g
fibre: 7.1g	Sodium:2.4g

Smoked mackerel scotch eggs

Prep time: 35 minutes
Cook time: 25 minutes

Serves 4Ingredients

- 200g hot-smoked peppered mackerel fillet
- A small handful of chives, finely sliced
- 50g full-fat cream cheese
- 2 tsp horseradish sauce
- Finely grated zest ½ lemon, plus a squeeze of juice
- 300g cooked mashed potato
- 4 medium free-range eggs
- Sunflower oil for deep-frying

For the coating

- 100g plain flour
- 2 medium free-range eggs, beaten
- 150g coarse fresh white breadcrumbs

Preparation Instructions

1. The mackerel's skin should be peeled off and cut into pieces. Put the chunks in the bowl of a food processor, along with the chives, cream cheese, horseradish, lemon zest, and lemon juice. Pulse several times to break down the mackerel. Add the mashed potato and pulse again to combine. Avoid overworking it. Add some salt and pepper to the mixture, then chill in the refrigerator.

2. Bring a pan of water to a boil, add the 4 eggs and cook for 6½ minutes. When the eggs are cool enough to handle, drain them and run them under a cold tap (this also stops them from cooking further). Shell them with care.

3. The mackerel mixture should be divided into 8 equal sections. Each portion should then be formed into a rough disc with a diameter of 6 cm. Put a disc in your palm, place a boiled egg in the middle, and then cover it with another disc. Mould the smoked mackerel and potato around the egg, sealing the joins well. Repeat this process with the remaining eggs and discs.

4. Prepare three small dishes For the coating. Sprinkle salt and pepper over the flour in a bowl. Then, pour the beaten eggs in. Tip the breadcrumbs into the third. Add seasoned flour to each scotch egg and coat it. Roll it in the breadcrumbs before dipping it in the beaten egg. Chill the eggs until you're ready to cook them.

5. On a digital thermometer, heat a deep pan with 5-7 cm of sunflower oil to 175°C, or until the oil is hot enough to turn a few breadcrumbs golden in 30–40 seconds. Lower the coated eggs into the oil, a couple at a time, and fry them for 6-8 minutes, turning regularly until golden and crisp all over. Drain on kitchen paper and leave to cool before eating.

Nutritional values Per Serving:

Calories: 544
fat: 31.6gg
protein: 27g
carbs: 37.1g
fibre: 1.4g
Sodium:1.8g

One-pan English breakfast frittata

Prep time: 10 minutes
Cook time: 25-30 minutes
Serves 4

Ingredients

- 300g new potatoes, sliced
- 2 tbsp olive oil
- 6 streaky bacon rashers, chopped
- 8 chipolatas
- A bunch of spring onions, sliced

- 12 cherry tomatoes
- 8 large free-range eggs
- Handful grated Cheddar

Preparation Instructions :

1. Preheat the grill to medium-high heat. Cook the potatoes in a pan of boiling salted water for 4-5 minutes, then drain. Heat the oil in a large frying pan and gently fry the potatoes for 5 minutes. Take out and place aside.
2. Turn up the heat, fry the bacon for 5 minutes, until crisp, and add to the potatoes. Fry the sausages in the bacon fat over medium heat for 5-6 minutes until cooked through.
3. Add the spring onions, cherry tomatoes, and potatoes back to the pan. The eggs should be lightly whisked in a jug with plenty of seasoning before being added to the pan. The frittata should be cooked for 6-7 minutes over low heat, or until almost set, then topped with cheese and placed under the grill for 5 minutes to finish setting and browning the top. Serve with toast and relish.

Nutritional Value Per Serving :

Calories: 567   fat: 41.5g
protein: 33g   carbs:18g
fibre: 2.8g   Sodium:2.8g

Big breakfast Yorkshire pudding

Prep time: 15 minutes
Cook time: 1 hour
Serves 2-4

Ingredients

- 4 British outdoor-bred pork sausages
- Olive oil for drizzling
- 200g small tomatoes on the vine
- 2 large portobello mushrooms
- 4 British outdoor-bred streaky bacon slices
- A few sprigs of fresh thyme
- 2 fresh rosemary sprigs, halved
- 2-4 medium free-range eggs

For the batter
- 140g plain flour
- 4 medium free-range eggs, beaten
- 200ml whole milk

Preparation Instructions :

1. To make the batter, whisk the flour and 4 beaten eggs in a bowl until smooth. Whisk while gradually adding the milk until smooth. Set aside after seasoning with salt and pepper.
2. Heat the oven to 200°C/180°C fan/gas 6. Place the sausages in a roasting pan, top with olive oil, season, and roast for 15 minutes or until gently browned. Add the tomatoes and mushrooms to the tin, cover the mushrooms with the bacon, drizzle a little oil from the tin's bottom, and then season to taste.
3. Increase the oven to 220°C/200°C fan/gas 7. Return the tin to the oven for 10 minutes, then remove it and pour in the batter. Put the tin straight back in the oven for 25-30 minutes until the batter is puffed up and golden. Crack the remaining eggs into low spots in the pudding, then return it to the oven for 6-8 minutes or until the whites are set and the yolks are still runny. Serve hot.

Nutritional Value Per Serving :

Calories: 629
fat: 39g
protein: 36.6g
carbs:31.7g
fibre: 2.7g
Sodium:1.8g

Blueberry waffles with maple butter

Prep time: 25 minutes
Cook time:
Serves 4

Ingredients

- 175g plain flour
- ¼ tsp bicarb soda
- ½ tsp baking powder
- 1 tbsp icing sugar
- 1 tsp ground cinnamon, plus extra to serve
- 300ml buttermilk
- 50ml whole milk
- 50g unsalted butter, melted and cooled, plus extra to grease
- 2 medium free-range eggs, separated
- 300g blueberries

For the whipped maple butter
- 150g unsalted butter
- 4 tbsp maple syrup, plus extra to serve

You'll also need
- A waffle iron or ridged griddle pan

Preparation Instructions :

1. Melt the butter for the whipped butter in a small saucepan over medium heat. Continue to cook, stirring regularly, until the butter turns brown and smells nutty. Pour into a bowl and add the maple syrup, then chill until the butter re-solidifies but is still soft (about 30 minutes). Beat the butter using an electric hand mixer until very pale and fluffy. Stir in a pinch of sea salt, then set aside at room temperature until ready to serve.
2. Grease an 18cm waffle iron and heat to high. Sift the flour, bicarb, baking powder, icing sugar, and cinnamon together in a large bowl. In another bowl, whisk the buttermilk, milk, butter, and egg yolks, then pour into the dry ingredients and mix until just combined.
3. Whisk the egg whites to firm peaks using an electric hand mixer, then fold them into the waffle batter, followed by half the blueberries. Ladle about ¼ of the batter into the middle of the waffle iron and cook for 6-8 minutes until crisp and golden. Cook the remaining batter while maintaining the warm waffles in a low oven.

Nutritional Value Per Serving :

Calories: 594
fat: 35.2g
protein: 12.1g
carbs: 55.7g
fibre: 3.3g
Sodium:0.5g

Scotch woodcock

Prep time: 10 minutes
Serves 1

Ingredients

- 1-2 slices of bread, toasted
- Knob of butter, plus extra to spread
- Patum Peperium The Gentleman's Relish
- 2 medium free-range eggs, beaten and seasoned
- 1 tsp crème fraîche
- 1 tsp drained capers in brine (optional)
- 1-2 anchovies, drained and sliced in half lengthways
- Snipped chives or chopped parsley to serve

Preparation Instructions :

1. Toast the bread and spread it with butter and The Gentleman's Relish while it's still warm.
2. In a nonstick frying pan, melt some butter. Add the beaten eggs once it begins to foam, then simmer over low heat. The uncooked egg should flow down the bottom of the pan to set. Use a wooden spoon or spatula

to gently fold the eggs as they set to form soft curds.

3. When the scrambled eggs are almost cooked (they should still be slightly wet/runny in places as they'll continue to cook in the heat of the pan), remove them from the heat and stir in the crème fraîche and capers, if using.

4. Place the anchovies on top of the scrambled eggs on the toast. To serve, add pepper and chives or parsley.

Nutritional Value Per Serving :

Calories: 414
fat:24.9g
protein: 22.7g
carbs: 24.1g
fibre: 1.6g
Sodium:2.2g

Easy huevos rancheros

Prep time: 20 minutes
Serves 2

Ingredients

- 400g in black or pinto beans, rinsed and drained (or 160g dried beans, soaked and boiled
- 1 tbsp sunflower oil for frying
- 4 small corn tortillas
- 2 medium free-range eggs
- 1 avocado, sliced
- 50g feta, crumbled (or queso fresco if you can find it)
- Hot sauce to serve (optional)

For the salsa ranchera

- 2 tbsp sunflower oil
- 1 small onion, finely chopped
- 1 jalapeño chili, seeds removed, sliced into matchsticks (plus extra, sliced, to serve – optional)
- 1/2 tsp ground cumin
- 1/2 tsp dried oregano

- 3 medium tomatoes, finely chopped (or use 6 tbsp chopped tinned tomatoes)
- Small bunch of coriander, chopped
- Juice 1/2 lime, plus wedges

Preparation Instructions :

1. For the salsa, heat the oil in a skillet over medium heat, then fry the onion and jalapeño until softened (about 4 minutes). Add the cumin, oregano, and tomatoes, then cook for 3 minutes or until the mixture becomes saucy. Stir in half the coriander and season with some salt. For five minutes, simmer with the lid on and the heat on low. Season with lime juice.

2. Meanwhile, put the beans and a splash of water in a pan and warm over low-medium heat until hot. Mash until mostly smooth with a little texture.

3. Heat the oil, then briefly fry the tortillas on both sides until just toasted. Drain on kitchen paper. Fry the eggs in the same oil until cooked to your liking.

4. Add the eggs, beans, salsa, and feta to the tortillas before garnishing with the remaining coriander and avocado. Serve with lime wedges and additional jalapenos or hot sauce, if desired.

Nutritional Value Per Serving :

Calories: 595
fat: 39.5g
protein: 23.4g
carbs: 40.9g
Sodium:1.4g

Rich ham and cheese toastie

Prep time: 25 minutes
Serves 4

Ingredients

- 300ml whole milk
- 30g unsalted butter

- 30g plain flour
- 2 tsp dijon mustard
- 200g mature cheddar, grated
- 4 sourdough bread slices
- Olive oil to drizzle
- 100g parma ham slices
- Worcestershire sauce or hot chili sauce to finish

Preparation Instructions :

Heat the milk in a saucepan. Melt the butter in a different pan, then stir in the flour. Whisk in the hot milk and continue whisking as the sauce comes to a boil, then cook over medium heat for 2 minutes to cook out the flour (removing the flour's raw taste for a nuttier flavor). Take off the heat, then stir in the mustard and most of the cheddar, reserving about 70g.

2. Heat the grill to high. On a large baking sheet, arrange the sourdough and drizzle with olive oil. Grill toast until golden brown on one side. After flipping, add a layer of ham and a thin layer of cheese sauce over the bread. Cover with the remaining sauce, then sprinkle over the reserved cheddar.

3. Put back under the grill to melt the cheese. Drizzle with a little Worcestershire sauce or chili sauce – whichever you prefer – then serve immediately

Nutritional Value Per Serving :

Calories: 561
fat: 35.6g
protein: 26.6g
carbs: 32.7g
Fibre : 1.8g
Sodium:2.8g

Carrot cake waffles with orange mascarpone and candied walnuts

Prep time: 30 minutes
Serves 4-6

Ingredients

For the waffles
- 100g unsalted butter, plus extra to grease
- 250g plain flour
- 1 tbsp baking powder
- 1 tbsp light brown sugar
- 2 tsp mixed spice
- 2 medium free-range eggs
- 400ml whole milk
- 1 medium carrot, finely grated
- Maple syrup, honey, or golden syrup to serve

For the candied walnuts
- 50g walnut halves
- 5 tbsp maple syrup, honey, or golden syrup

For the orange mascarpone
- 250g mascarpone
- Finely grated zest 1 orange
- 2-3 tbsp icing sugar, sifted
- ½ tsp vanilla bean paste

You'll also need
- Waffle iron

Preparation Instructions :

1. For the candied walnuts, softly roast the nuts in a dry skillet over medium heat for 3–4 minutes. When the mixture has reduced to a sticky coating, add the maple syrup, honey, or golden syrup and heat while stirring for 3 to 4 minutes. Place the nuts on a lined tray, let them cool, and then coarsely slice them. Place aside.

2. For the orange mascarpone, combine all the ingredients in a bowl. Set aside until ready to use.

3. For the waffles, lightly grease a waffle

iron to high. The butter should be melted in a pan over medium heat, then cooked until foaming and smelling nutty. Pour the brown butter into a large bowl, and then leave it there for five minutes to cool. Whisk in the milk, eggs, sugar, baking powder, and spices after adding the flour and baking powder. Fold in the grated carrot.

4. Pour a ladleful of batter into the hot waffle iron, spreading to fill, then close and cook for 5-6 minutes until golden and cooked through. Set aside and repeat with the remaining batter, keeping the cooked waffles warm in a low oven.

5. Serve 1-2 waffles per person, topped with mascarpone, some candied walnuts, and an extra drizzle of maple syrup, honey, or golden syrup.

Nutritional Value Per Serving :

Calories: 637   fat: 43.8g
protein: 13.8g   carbs: 54.6g
Fibre : 2.7 g   Sodium:0.9g

One-pan potato latke with smoked salmon

Prep time: 30 minutes
Serves 4-6

Ingredients

- For the waffles
- 800g large starchy potatoes (we used russets), coarsely grated
- 1 medium onion, grated
- 3 tsp salt
- 4 tbsp matzo meal (or use matzo crackers, whizzed in a food processor until finely ground
- 1 medium egg, beaten
- Small bunch of chives, finely chopped
- 1 tsp caraway or cumin seeds, lightly crushed (optional)
- 4 tbsp light olive oil or vegetable oil
- 200g sustainable cold-smoked salmon slices to serve
- Sustainable salmon roe, finely chopped spring onion, dill sprigs, and lemon wedges to serve

For the herby crème fraîche

- 200g crème fraîche
- Small bunch of chives, finely chopped
- Small bunch of dill, finely chopped
- Finely grated zest 1 lemon

Preparation Instructions :

1. In a big bowl, combine the grated potatoes and onion with 2 teaspoons of salt. Mix well, then let out for 15 minutes to remove moisture.

2. Meanwhile, for the herby crème fraîche, mix all the ingredients in a bowl with some seasoning. Cover and chill until ready to serve.

3. Transfer the potato mixture to a clean tea towel or muslin square (discard any liquid in the bowl). Gather the edges together, then squeeze over the sink to remove as much moisture as you can (the potatoes need to be nice and dry so the latke crisps up). Return the mixture to the bowl and stir in the remaining salt and the matzo meal, egg, chives, caraway/cumin (if using), and plenty of black pepper. Mix to combine.

4. In a big frying pan (approximately 28 cm), heat 2 tbsp of oil over medium heat. Add the potato mixture to the skillet, pressing to spread it into an even layer. Don't worry if the edges are a little ragged – they'll turn extra crispy. Cook for 4-6 minutes, then carefully invert onto a plate. Heat the remaining oil in the pan, then slide the latke back in. Cook for an additional 4-6 minutes, or until golden on the other side.

5. Turn the latke out onto a serving board (or serve in the pan). Slice into wedges, then top with smoked salmon, herby crème

fraîche, salmon roe, spring onion, and dill sprigs, with lemon wedges for squeezing.

Nutritional Value Per Serving :

Calories: 441	fat: 26.1g
protein: 13.7g	carbs: 36g
Fibre : 3.9 g	Sodium:2.3g

Cheese croissant bread and butter pudding

Prep time: 15 minutes + Chilling
Serves 4-6

Ingredients

- Knob of soft butter for greasing the dish
- 6-8 croissants, depending on the size, ideally a day or two old
- 200g gruyère cheese, grated
- 150g ham hock, finely shredded
- 250ml whole milk
- 450ml double cream
- 3 medium free-range eggs and
- 2 egg yolks, lightly beaten
- 5 tbsp finely chopped chives (a 15g pack's worth)
- 2 tsp English mustard powder

You'll also need...

- 1.5l baking dish

Preparation Instructions :

1. Oven temperature set to 160°C fan/gas 4. Place the croissants on a baking sheet after cutting them in half horizontally. Put them in the oven for 5 minutes, then remove them to cool – you can turn off the oven now as you won't need it for a bit. This helps the croissants dry out so they'll greedily soak up the custard.
2. Arrange half the halved croissants, cut side up, in the baking dish. Scatter over half the cheese and all the ham, then arrange the rest of the halved croissants, cut side

down, on top.
3. Stir the milk and cream in a pan and warm until just steaming. Whisk in the eggs, yolks, chives, and mustard after turning the heat off, then season with salt and pepper. Slowly pour the mixture evenly over the croissants, then cover and chill for an hour or overnight. If you can, tilt the dish occasionally as you brush the custard onto the croissants to ensure that it is absorbed.
4. Reheat the oven to 160°C fan/gas 4. Take the dish out of the refrigerator, top it with the remaining cheese, place it on a baking sheet to catch any drips, and bake for a few minutes, or until the custard is just set and the cheese is bubbling (30-35 minutes). Before serving, let it settle for 5–10 minutes. Garnish with whatever you like (within reason).

Nutritional Value Per Serving :

Calories: 876	fat: 71.6g
protein: 28g	carbs: 28g
Fibre : 1.9 g	Sodium:1.8g

Sausage, chorizo, and red pepper rolls

Prep time: 15 minutes + Chilling
Serves 4-6

Ingredients

1 tbsp olive oil
- 4 British outdoor-reared pork sausages, cut in half lengthways
- 4 cooking chorizo sausages, cut in half lengthways
- 4 red or orange romano peppers, halved lengthways
- 4 ciabatta rolls, halved
- 1½ tbsp sherry vinegar or balsamic vinegar
- 4 tbsp mayonnaise (we used saffron mayo)
- 40g rocket

Preparation Instructions :

1. Set the oven's temperature to 220°C/200°C fan/gas 7. Heat the oil in a heavy roasting tin in the oven for 5 minutes. Add both types of sausage, cut side down, and roast for 5 minutes. Add the peppers, roast for 20 minutes, and then turn everything over.
2. Toast, warm or griddle the ciabatta rolls. Put the cooked sausages in a bowl with the vinegar, then stir well.
3. Spread the rolls with mayonnaise, then fill them with the rocket, sausages, and peppers, along with some juices from the roasting tin.

Nutritional Value Per Serving :

Calories: 755
fat: 52.7g
protein: 22.6g
carbs: 44.7g
Fibre : 5.3 g
Sodium:2.6g

Potato champ cakes with crispy bacon and fried eggs

Prep time: 30 minutes
Serves 4

Ingredients

- 750g floury potatoes(such as desired or maris-piper) peeled and cut into 4cm chunks
- 125ml semi-skimmed milk
- A bunch of spring onions, trimmed and finely sliced
- 2 tsp creamed horseradish, plus extra to serve (optional)
- 25g butter, cubed
- Plain flour for dusting
- 2 tbsp vegetable oil, plus a splash for frying
- 8 rashers British free-range smoked streaky bacon
- 4 medium free-range eggs
- Salad leaves to serve

Preparation Instructions :

1. Put the potatoes in a large pan, cover with cold salted water, bring to a boil, then simmer for 15 minutes until soft. After thoroughly draining, add the potatoes back to the empty pan. Allow to steam dry for a few minutes, then thoroughly mash.
2. Put the milk and spring onions in a small pan in the meantime. Bring to a simmer and cook for 1-2 minutes. Mix the mashed potato with the horseradish, butter, and plenty of salt and pepper to make a stiff mash. Set aside and, when cool enough to handle, shape into 8 equal patties (flour your hands to prevent sticking).
3. Set the oven to warm. Heat half the oil in a non-stick frying pan over medium heat, then add 4 champ cakes and fry for about 3 minutes on each side until golden brown and heated through. Transfer to a baking tray and keep warm in the oven while you add the remaining oil and fry the rest of the cakes.
4. Wipe out the pan and add a splash of oil, then cook the bacon for a few minutes on each side until crisp. Move the bacon to the edges of the pan, then fry the eggs in the bacon fat until they're cooked to your liking.
5. Divide the champ cakes, bacon, and fried eggs among 4 plates. Serve with salad and a little extra horseradish on the side, if you like.

Nutritional Value Per Serving :

Calories: 532
fat: 30.8g
protein: 21.2g
carbs: 40.4g
Fibre : 4.4g
Sodium:1.7g

Wild garlic, tarragon, and mint roast chicken with lettuce and peas

Prep time: 20 minutes
Cook time: 1 hour and 15 min
Serves 4-6

Ingredients

- 0g butter, softened
- ½ bunch of wild garlic leaves, finely chopped
- 1 tbsp each fresh tarragon and mint leaves, finely chopped
- 2kg free-range chicken, at room temperature
- Steamed potatoes to serve

For the lettuce and peas
- 25g unsalted butter
- 340g jar sweet silverskin pickled onions, drained
- 300ml vegetable stock
- 400g frozen peas
- 2 baby gem lettuces, sliced
- 2 tbsp crème fraîche
- Small handful of mint leaves, torn
- Useful to have
- Probe thermometer

Preparation Instructions :

1. Oven temperature set at 180°C fan/gas 6. Butter, wild garlic, and herbs are combined with salt and pepper. Use your hand to carefully pull the skin covering the breast away from the chicken's neck end. Spread two-thirds of the butter mixture over the breast, under the skin, then rub the rest over the skin. Season, put the bird in a roasting tin, and roast for 1¼ hours, basting every 15 minutes, or until the juices run clear when a skewer is pushed into the thickest part of the thigh or it reads 70-72°C on a probe thermometer. Rest for 10 minutes (the core temperature will rise a little)

2. Meanwhile melt the 25g butter in a large pan. Add the pickled onions and cook over medium heat for 5 minutes until softened.

3. Add the stock and peas, bring to a boil, then cook for 3 minutes. Add the lettuce, cook for 2 minutes, then stir in the crème fraîche, mint, and some seasoning.

4. Steamed potatoes should be served on the side, along with any leftover cooking fluids from the chicken, lettuce, and peas.

Nutritional Value Per Serving :

Calories: 460
fat: 23.1g
protein: 52g
carbs: 9.2g
Fibre : 3.9g
Sodium:1.2g

Pimm's glazed chicken with strawberry and cucumber salad

Prep time: 25-30 minutes + 4 Hours Marinating
Serves 4-6

Ingredients

- 8 bone-in free-range chicken thighs
- 2 tbsp Pimm's No. 1
- 1 tbsp tamari or soy sauce
- 1 garlic clove, crushed
- 2 tsp grated fresh ginger

- 1 tsp brown sugar
- 1 tsp white miso paste

For the Pimm's glaze
- 100ml Pimm's No. 1
- 2 tbsp orange marmalade
- 2 tbsp dark brown sugar
- 1 tbsp cider vinegar
- 1 tsp white miso paste

For the strawberry and cucumber salad
- 300g strawberries, sliced
- 1 cucumber, diced
- ½ small red onion, finely diced
- Small bunch of basil, leaves picked
- 2 tbsp extra-virgin olive oil
- 1 tbsp Pimm's No. 1
- 2 tsp each lemon, lime, and orange juice
- 1 tsp sugar

Preparation Instructions :

1. Place the chicken in a bowl with the 2 tbsp Pimm's, tamari, garlic, ginger, brown sugar, and miso. Toss, then cover and marinate for 2-4 hours in the fridge.

2. Put all the ingredients for the glaze in a small pan and heat over medium heat to dissolve the sugar. Bring to a boil, then reduce heat and simmer for 5 to 6 minutes, or until thick and syrupy. Reserve for cooling.

3. Heat the barbecue for direct heat (arrange the coals in the center). 30 minutes before cooking, remove the chicken from the refrigerator. Take out the marinade and blot it dry with paper towels. Grill the chicken with the lid down for 20-25 minutes, turning and basting with glaze regularly, until golden and sticky and cooked through (the juices should run clear when pierced with a skewer and a digital thermometer should read 72ºC). Set the chicken aside to rest while you prepare the salad.

4. For the salad, combine all the ingredients in a large bowl. Serve the chicken drizzled with extra glaze with the salad on the side.

Nutritional Value Per Serving :
Calories: 278
fat: 11.3g
protein: 18.1g
carbs: 19.3g
Fibre : 2.6g
Sodium:0.7g

Duck and sausage cassoulet

SIMMERING TIME 1½ HOURS, OVEN TIME 1 HOUR 50-55 MIN, PLUS OVERNIGHT SOAKING
Serves 8

Ingredients
- 500g haricot beans, soaked overnight
- 2 onions, 1 halved, 1 finely chopped
- 4 bay leaves
- 4 fresh thyme sprigs, plus extra to garnish
- 4 fresh rosemary sprigs
- 1 garlic bulb, separated into cloves
- 4 confit duck legs, fat reserved
- 6 outdoor reared Toulouse sausages (or good quality pork sausages)
- 1 carrot, finely chopped
- 1 celery stick, finely chopped
- 200g smoked bacon lardons
- 2 tbsp tomato purée
- Large handful of fresh flatleaf parsley, chopped
- 200ml dry white wine
- 500ml chicken stock, hot, plus an extra splash if needed
- 30g gruyère cheese, grated
- 50g fresh breadcrumbs

Preparation Instructions :

1. Drain the beans, then transfer to a large heavy-based pan with the onion halves, 2 of the bay leaves, 2 thyme sprigs, half the rosemary, and all but 4 garlic cloves (no need to peel). Pour over water to cover,

bring to a boil, then simmer for 1½ hours until the beans are just tender. Drain and discard the onion, herbs, and garlic.

2. Meanwhile, heat a deep hob-safe casserole over high heat, add the duck legs, and fry skin-side down for 5 minutes until crisp. Set aside on a baking tray and pour off most of the fat in the casserole.

3. The sausages should be added to the casserole and cooked for 5 minutes in the duck fat to brown all sides. Duck legs should be cut in half and put aside.

4. Heat the oven to 140°C/120°C fan/gas 1. Add the chopped onion, carrot, celery, and lardons to the hot casserole, then cook, stirring occasionally, for 10 minutes until the veg is soft and the lardons are golden.

5. Peel the reserved garlic cloves and add to the casserole with the tomato purée and parsley, then cook for a minute. Pour the wine in, bring to a simmer, and cook until it has been reduced by around half. Season well after stirring in the stock, the remaining herbs, and the cooked beans.

6. Return the duck, skin-side up, and sausages to the casserole along with any resting juices, stirring them into the beans, then put in the oven and bake for 1½ hours. Check halfway through, adding a little more stock if the cassoulet looks dry.

7. Sprinkle the shredded cheese and breadcrumbs over the top of the dish after combining them with salt and pepper.

8. Cassoulet should be baked for an additional 20 to 25 minutes for a beautiful brown top. Spread more thyme on top when serving.

Nutritional Value Per Serving :

Calories: 656	fat: 27.8g
protein: 46.3g	carbs: 42.1g
Fibre : 17.3g	Sodium:2.2g

Summer chicken tray bake

Prep time: 5-10 minutes
Cook time: 40-45 min
Serves 4

Ingredients

- 600g new potatoes
- 4 garlic cloves
- 8 free-range chicken thighs
- 2 tbsp olive oil
- 2 courgettes
- 200g cherry vine tomatoes
- 150g pesto

Preparation Instructions :

1. Set the oven's temperature to 220°C/200°C fan/gas 7. Peel the garlic cloves and cut the young potatoes in half. Place the potatoes and garlic around the chicken thighs in a big roasting pan. Drizzle over the olive oil and season with salt and pepper, then roast for 40-45 minutes.

2. Meanwhile, slice the courgettes. When the chicken has been in the oven for 20 minutes, add the courgettes to the roasting tin.

3. For the final 10 minutes of the cooking time, add the tomatoes to the tin.

4. Add the pesto and serve the chicken after it has turned golden and is fully cooked.

Nutritional Value Per Serving :

Calories: 468
fat: 22.1g
protein: 36.6g
carbs: 26.2g
Fibre : 3.6g
Sodium:0.8g

Duck breasts with butter beans and creamy apple slaw

Prep time: 30 minutes
Cook time:10 min
Serves 4

Ingredients

- 4 x free-range duck breasts, skin scored
- 300g banana shallots, sliced
- 300g carrots, cut into 2cm chunks
- 4 garlic cloves, crushed
- 2 small apples, quartered, cored, and sliced into matchsticks
- 150g half-fat crème fraîche
- Juice 1 lemon
- 600ml chicken or light beef stock
- 2 x 400g cans of butter beans, drained and rinsed
- 100g watercress

Preparation Instructions :

1. Heat the oven to 200°C/180°C fan/gas 6. Over medium-high heat, place the duck breasts skin-side down in a large, heavy-based ovenproof pan. Cook for about 8 minutes to brown the skin and render the fat. Turn the duck over, transfer to the oven and cook for 8-12 minutes, depending on whether you like it rare or medium. Transfer the duck breasts to a plate and set aside.

2. Return the pan to the stovetop over medium heat after removing the majority of the duck fat from it. Cook the carrots and shallots for 10 minutes, or until they are tender and lightly brown, then add the garlic and cook for one more minute.

3. Mix the apple, crème fraîche, and half the lemon juice in the meantime.

4. Add the stock to the pan, bring to a boil, then add the butter beans and simmer until the liquid has reduced by a third – about 10 minutes. Season with salt, pepper, and lemon juice to taste.

5. Slice the rested duck, return to the pan, along with any resting juices, and serve with the apple slaw and watercress on the side.

Nutritional Value Per Serving :

Calories: 640
fat: 22.8g
protein: 62g
carbs: 31.9g
Fibre : 14.6g
Sodium:0.7g

Roast chicken thighs with new potatoes and greens

Prep time: 15 minutes
Cook time:40-50 min
Serves 6

Ingredients

- 500g new potatoes, halved if large
- 1 red onion, cut into wedges
- 1 leek, chopped
- 2 garlic cloves, crushed
- 1 tbsp olive oil
- 6 free-range skin-on, bone-in chicken thighs
- 150g kale, shredded
- 200ml good-quality chicken stock
- 1-2 tbsp sherry vinegar
- A few fresh thyme sprigs (optional)

Preparation Instructions :

1. Heat the oven to 200°C/180°C fan/gas 6. Toss the potatoes, onion, leek, and garlic with the oil in a large roasting tin. Add the chicken on top and season with a healthy dose of black pepper and a pinch of salt. For 40 minutes, roast.

2. Put the tin back in the oven for the

remaining cooking time, toss in the greens, and then add the stock. Once the chicken and potatoes are done and browned, return them to the oven for a further 5 to 10 minutes.

3. Add the vinegar to the tin and mix it with the cooking juices for an easy gravy. Taste and season. If desired, add some thyme to the mixture.

Nutritional Value Per Serving :

Calories: 223	fat: 7.8g
protein: 20.2g	carbs: 16g
Fibre : 3.9g	Sodium:0.3g

garlic and fry for another minute.

2. Add the chicken, gravy, and crème fraîche and bring to a boil. Simmer for 5 minutes until thickened slightly. Stir in the spinach and allow it to wilt for 30 seconds. Use to fill 8 pancakes, roll them up and lay in an ovenproof dish, top with the cheese, and bake for 15-20 minutes until golden. Serve with a salad.

Nutritional Value Per Serving :

Calories: 954	fat: 58.1g
protein: 52.5g	carbs: 52.7g
Sodium:5.4g	

Creamy chicken, spinach, and pancetta pancakes

Prep time: 10 minutes
Cook time:30-35 min
Serves 4

Ingredients

- 1 tbsp olive oil, plus extra for greasing
- 1 onion, chopped
- 100g pancetta or streaky bacon, chopped
- 200g chestnut mushrooms, sliced
- 1 garlic clove, chopped
- 400g portion cooked, shredded chicken
- 300ml ready-made gravy or stock
- 200g crème fraîche
- 100g baby spinach
- 8 ready-made thin pancakes (or make your own with this recipe for perfect pancakes)
- 75g mature Cheddar, grated

Preparation Instructions :

1. Set the oven's temperature to 200°C/ fan180°C/gas 6. In a deep frying pan, gently heat the oil. Add the onion and pancetta, and cook for 3 to 4 minutes, or until golden. Add the mushrooms, turn up the heat and fry for 3-4 minutes. Add the

Roast chicken with lemon, garlic, and thyme

Prep time: 45 minutes
Cook time: 1 hour and 30 min
Serves 4

Ingredients

- 1 whole chicken, about 1.6kg
- ½ lemon
- 8 fresh thyme sprigs (or 2 fresh rosemary sprigs)
- 4 bay leaves
- 2 onions, peeled and halved
- 5 garlic cloves
- 1 tbsp olive oil

For the potatoes

- 1kg baby new potatoes, scrubbed and halved
- 5 garlic cloves
- Handful of fresh thyme sprigs (or oregano or rosemary), leaves picked
- 4 tbsp olive oil

For the gravy

- ½ chicken stock cube
- 1 tbsp plain flour
- 150ml dry white wine

Preparation Instructions :

1. Heat the oven to its highest setting. Inside and out, season the chicken before stuffing it with the lemon, half the herbs, and half the onion. Roughly slice the remaining onions, spread them over the base of a roasting tin, then scatter over the garlic and the remaining herbs. Rub the chicken with the oil and season generously with salt and pepper.

2. Pull the legs slightly away from the body, then sit the chicken, breast-side down, on top of the onions, and put the tin in the oven. Immediately turn down the heat to 190°C/170°C fan/gas 5 and cook for just over an hour (30 minutes per kg, plus 15 minutes for good measure). The chicken is cooked when the juices from the thickest part of the thigh run clear when pierced with a skewer.

3. Put the potatoes, garlic, and herbs on a big baking sheet, drizzle with oil, season everything thoroughly, and roast the chicken at the same time. Roast the chicken in the oven, stirring occasionally and adding a little oil if they look a bit dry. In approximately an hour, they will be crisp and golden.

4. For the most succulent meat, it's essential to rest the bird in a warm place, covered in foil, for 15 minutes while you make the gravy. For the gravy, skim off most of the fat from the chicken and discard, leaving only a few tablespoons behind. Put the tin on the hob over medium heat. Crumble in the stock cube, whisk in the flour and leave to bubble for a few minutes. Whisk in the wine a little at a time, letting it bubble for a minute between each addition, then boil for a few moments before adding enough boiling water to thin the gravy to your desired consistency (add 200ml-400ml water, depending on how thick you like your gravy). Simmer for 5-10 minutes, then taste and season; I like lots of salt and pepper in my gravy.

5. Remove the herbs and throw them away, but keep the tasty onions and garlic to go with the chicken. The gravy should be poured through a sieve into a heated jug. Place the potatoes, onions, and garlic around the chicken on a large platter or in a large dish. Bring the bird to the table, carve it, and serve.

Nutritional Value Per Serving :

Calories: 664	fat: 23.1g
protein: 62.1g	carbs: 42.6g
Fibre : 5.1g	Sodium:5.4g

Lemon thyme roast chicken and bread sauce stuffed onions

Prep time: 30 minutes
Cook time: 1 hour and 15 min
Serves 4-6

Ingredients

- 60g unsalted butter, softened
- A bunch fresh lemon thyme leaves finely chopped
- 2kg free-range chicken, at room temperature
- 1 lemon, halved
- Olive oil for rubbing/brushing
- 4 unpeeled garlic cloves, bashed
- 200ml white wine
- For the stuffed onions
- 6 medium onions, unpeeled
- 200ml whole milk
- 15g butter
- 6 cloves
- 6 black peppercorns
- 2 fresh bay leaves
- 2 garlic cloves, bashed
- 100g fresh breadcrumbs
- 2 tbsp single cream
- Pinch freshly grated nutmeg

- 30g panko breadcrumbs

You'll also need
- Kitchen string
- 6-hole muffin tray or roasting tin just large enough to fit the onions

Useful to have
- Probe thermometer

Preparation Instructions :

1. Oven temperature set to 160°C fan/gas 4. Season the butter while combining the thyme. At the neck end of the chicken, loosen the skin over the breast, then spread the breast under the skin with the butter mixture. Put a lemon half inside the cavity and tie the legs with string. Rub oil over the skin and add more seasoning. Put the chicken in a roasting tin with the garlic, wine and the other lemon half. Roast, basting every 15 minutes, for 1¼ hours or until the juices run clear when a skewer is pushed into the thickest part of the thigh or a thermometer reads 70-72°C.

2. For ten minutes, let the chicken lay on a board (the temperature will rise a little as it rests). To prepare gravy, strain the cooking juices into a small pan and heat them quickly over medium-low. Add seasoning to taste.

3. In the meantime, heat a large pan of salted water to a boil before adding the onions. Return to a boil, then simmer for 10 minutes until tender. Drain and, when cool enough to handle, slice 2cm off the tops and trim the bases flat. Scoop out the core of each onion, leaving 2-3 layers intact. Half of the onion should be finely chopped and set aside.

4. When the milk, butter, cloves, peppercorns, bay leaves, and garlic are steaming, remove from the heat and let the infusion sit for 20 minutes.

5. In a small pan, strain the infused milk (discard the solids). Fresh breadcrumbs and diced onion should be added. Cook for 3 to 4 minutes on medium heat, stirring often. Stir in the cream, nutmeg, and seasoning.

6. Divide the bread sauce among the onion shells. Brush the skin of each onion with olive oil, then put it in the muffin tray/roasting tin. Sprinkle with the panko breadcrumbs, drizzle with a little oil, then roast in the tray/tin alongside the chicken for the final 30 minutes of the cooking time.

7. Carve the chicken and serve the stuffed onions and gravy alongside your favourite veg.

Nutritional Value Per Serving :

Calories: 565	fat: 22.2g
protein: 54.5g	carbs: 29.1g
Fibre : 3.3g	Sodium:0.8g

Spatchcock duck with plums and redcurrants

Prep time: 45 minutes
PLUS RESTING AND 12-24 HOURS BRINING
Serves 2-4

Ingredients
- Free-range duck (about 2kg)
- 6 tarragon sprigs
- 4 thyme sprigs
- 2 tbsp salt flakes
- 2 tsp dark brown sugar
- Finely grated zest ½ orange
- 4-6 plums, halved or quartered
- 150g redcurrants
- 60ml Madeira (or orange juice)
- 1 cinnamon stick
- 1-star anise
- 1 fresh bay leaf
- 3 tbsp runny honey
- 3 tbsp good balsamic vinegar

You'll also need
- Oven tray and wire rack
- BBQ with a lid
- Large old flameproof roasting tin

- Small roasting tin or cast-iron skillet

Useful to have
- Digital probe thermometer

Preparation Instructions :

1. Place the duck on a cutting board with the breast facing down the day before you plan to eat. Cut both sides of the backbone from the neck to the tail using a pair of precise kitchen shears. Turn the duck over and flatten it by pressing down firmly with the heel of your palm across the breastbone. Place the duck in the sink on a wire rack. Put the duck on a wire rack and sit it in the sink. Pour a kettle of boiling water over the duck, then pat dry and use a skewer to prick the skin all over, being careful not to puncture the flesh.

2. Finely chop the leaves from 3 tarragon sprigs and 2 thyme sprigs, then mix with the salt, sugar, orange zest and some black pepper. Rub the mixture all over the duck skin and flesh. Put the duck on a wire rack set over an oven tray and put in the bottom of the fridge, uncovered, to marinate for 12-24 hours.

3. When ready to cook, heat a barbeque for low-medium indirect heat (place the coals around the barbecue's sides, leaving a space for the old roasting tin; if your BBQ has a thermometer, you want it to be around 150°C). Take the duck out of the fridge 45 minutes before cooking. Place the old tin on the grill's base to catch any duck grease before placing the duck, breast-side down, right over the tin. 2 hours of roasting with the cover off.

4. Duck should be taken from the grill and put aside. To increase the temperature (which should be around 200oC), stoke the coals. In a small roasting pan or cast-iron skillet, combine the plums, red currants, Madeira or orange juice, spices, and additional herbs while the duck is resting. After seasoning, place the pan or tin on the grill over the fire with the lid down. Roast the plums for 20 to 25 minutes, or until they are tender and the sauce has reduced and bubbled.

5. Mix the honey and balsamic vinegar in a small bowl and brush all over the duck. Put the duck, skin-side up, back on the center of the grill (over indirect heat). Cook with the lid down for 20-25 minutes, basting the skin with the rest of the glaze, until sticky and caramelized. Set aside to rest in a warm place for about 20 minutes before carving.

Nutritional Value Per Serving :

Calories: 761
fat: 41.3g
protein: 75g
carbs: 16.8g
Fibre : 2.7g
Sodium:2.6g

Chicken stew with lemon and herb crumb topping

Prep time: 30 minutes
SIMMERING TIME 45 MIN
Serves 6

Ingredients
- Olive oil for frying
- 6 banana shallots, halved
- 6 skinless, boneless free-range chicken thighs, chopped
- 2 garlic cloves, crushed
- 25g butter
- 2 tbsp plain flour
- 250ml dry white wine
- 600ml chicken stock, hot
- 1 large fresh rosemary sprig, leaves removed and chopped
- 1 tbsp chopped fresh thyme leaves
- 600g chantenay carrots
- Crusty bread to serve (optional)

- For the herb crumb topping
- 50g dried breadcrumbs
- Zest ½ lemon
- Handful of fresh parsley, chopped

You'll also need...
- Large casserole with a lid

Preparation Instructions :

1. The shallots should be gently fried for 10 minutes, covered, with a small amount of oil in the casserole, and stirred now and then.
2. In the meantime, heat a generous amount of oil in a big frying pan over medium heat. The chicken should be fried for 5 to 6 minutes until browned, and then transferred to a platter.
3. Add the garlic and butter to the casserole and cook for a further. Stir in the flour and cook for 1 minute, then add the wine and bubble to evaporate most of it. Stir in the stock, bring to a boil, then add the browned chicken with the rosemary, thyme, and carrots.
4. Turn the heat to low, cover, and simmer for 45 minutes.
5. Meanwhile, combine all the ingredients for the herb crumb topping and season. Divide two-thirds of the stew among 6 bowls, sprinkle with the topping, then serve with crusty bread, if you like.

Nutritional Value Per Serving :

Calories: 281
fat: 10.3g
protein: 18.8g
carbs: 18.4g
Fibre : 4.9g
Sodium:0.7g

Chicken and vegetable traybake

Prep time: 10 minutes
Cook time: 35 min oven
Serves 2

Ingredients

- 100g celeriac, cut into 1cm chunks
- 1 red onion, chopped into wedges
- 2 tsp olive oil
- 2 boneless, skinless free-range chicken thighs (about 90g each), cut in half
- Finely grated zest and juice 1 lemon
- 1 red pepper, sliced
- 8 tender stem broccoli stalks, halved lengthways if thick
- 2 tbsp chopped fresh mint and flatleaf parsley to serve

Preparation Instructions :

1. Heat the oven to 200°C/180°C fan/gas 6. In a roasting pan, combine the carrot, celeriac, and onion with 12 teaspoon of oil. Season to taste. Combine the chicken with a further 1/2 tsp of oil and the lemon zest in a bowl, and then lay it with the red pepper slices on top of the veggies. For 25 minutes, roast.
2. When the chicken is thoroughly cooked and the vegetables are soft, add the broccoli to the roasting pan, stir everything together, and roast for an additional 10 minutes. Taste the dish, then season to taste with lemon juice. To serve, scatter the freshly chopped herbs over top and add the final 1 tsp of oil.

Nutritional Value Per Serving :

Calories: 240	fat: 6g
protein: 26g	carbs: 16g
Fibre : 9g	Sodium:0.3g

Chapter 3: Fish and Seafood

Whole roast plaice with anchovy and sage butter, new potatoes, and sea vegetables

Prep time: 30 minutes
Cook time: 50-55 min oven
Serves 2

Ingredients

- 500g new potatoes, cut into 1cm rounds
- Olive oil to drizzle
- Sea salt flakes
- 2 lemons, 1 thinly sliced, ½ juiced, and ½ cut into wedges to serve
- 75g butter, plus an extra knob for frying
- 3 fresh sage sprigs, leaves finely chopped, a few reserved wholes
- 5 anchovy fillets in oil, drained and chopped
- 160g mixed sea vegetables
- 1 large sustainable whole plaice

Preparation Instructions :

1. Heat the oven to 180°C/160°C fan/gas 4. Toss the potatoes in a large roasting tin with a good drizzle of oil and season with sea salt and black pepper. Nestle the lemon slices among the potatoes, then roast for 40 minutes, turning halfway through, until golden and crisp.
2. Meanwhile, melt the 75g butter in a sauté pan over low-medium heat and fry the reserved whole sage leaves until crisp, then drain on kitchen paper and set aside. Gently heat the butter in the pan until it begins to brown and smell nutty (don't let it burn). Add a little lemon juice (be careful as it may spit), then stir in the anchovies and chopped sage. Cook for another minute or so until the anchovies start to break down and the sage turns crisp, then transfer to a bowl and keep warm. Don't wash the pan.
3. Once the potatoes are crisp, lay the whole plaice on top and drizzle with a tablespoon of the anchovy butter. Bake for 10-15 minutes until the fish is just cooked. When you insert a small knife, the delicate flesh should be opaque and flaky.
4. Heat a small knob of butter in the sauté pan and add the sea vegetables. Cook, stirring, for 3 minutes until wilted, then season with salt and lemon juice.
5. Once the plaice is cooked, arrange the sea veg around the fish, scatter with the fried sage leaves and drizzle with the remaining anchovy butter. Serve with lemon wedges.

Nutritional Value Per Serving :

Calories: 763   fat: 51g
protein: 33g   carbs: 40.7g
Fibre : 4.5g   Sodium:3.7g

Mackerel with potato hash

Prep time: 15 minutes
Cook time: 10 min
Serves 4

Ingredients

- 4 frozen sustainable mackerel fillets, defrosted
- 2 tbsp olive oil
- 150g frozen chopped shallots
- 10 frozen roast potatoes, defrosted and roughly chopped
- 50g frozen petit pois
- Grated zest and juice 1 lemon

- 25g fresh flat-leaf parsley, chopped
- 25g fresh dill, chopped, plus extra to serve
- Greek yogurt to serve

Preparation Instructions :

1. Heat the grill to medium. Place the mackerel fillets skin-side up on the grill tray, top with 1 tablespoon oil, and generously sprinkle with salt and pepper. Just done after 10 minutes on the grill.
2. Meanwhile, heat the remaining 1 tbsp oil in a large frying pan and fry the shallots until softened and golden. Add the potatoes and turn up the heat, tossing the potatoes and shallots to brown slightly (they should start to break down a little).
3. Add the petit pois and lemon juice, then toss through to cook gently.

Stir in the chopped herbs and the lemon zest, then season with salt and pepper. Divide among 4 plates, then top each with a mackerel fillet and generous dollops of yogurt. Scatter over extra dill to serve.

Nutritional Value Per Serving :

Calories: 575	fat: 33.5g
protein: 19.9g	carbs: 47.4g
Fibre : 2g	Sodium:0.8g

Chilli and garlic prawns with sea purslane

Prep time: 20 minutes
Serves 4

Ingredients

- 100g wild sea purslane, available from Abel & Cole
- 2 good glugs of extra-virgin olive oil
- 3 garlic cloves, unpeeled, bashed with a rolling pin
- 1 tsp chilli flakes
- 800g large sustainable raw shell-on tiger or king prawns
- Grated zest and juice 1 lemon, plus wedges to serve
- 100ml good quality dry white wine
- Fresh baguette or sourdough to serve

Preparation Instructions :

1. Pull the purslane leaves from the stalks; discard the woody stalks.
2. Heat the oil in a wide frying pan and add the garlic, chili, and sea purslane. Fry for 1 minute, then add the prawns. Cook for 2 minutes on each side until bright pink, then add the lemon zest, juice, and white wine. Turn up the heat and simmer briskly for 3 minutes. Don't cook off all the wine, as acidity is key to this dish.
3. Remove from the heat and serve straight from the pan with hunks of fresh crusty baguette or sourdough.

Nutritional Value Per Serving :

Calories: 263	fat: 10.2g
protein: 36.5g	carbs: 1g
Fibre : 1.6g	Sodium:1.2g

Tomato and basil mackerel bake

Prep time: 25 minutes
Cook time: 20-25 min
Serves 4

Ingredients

- 250g large pasta shells
- 1 head of broccoli
- Glug of oil
- 2 finely sliced red onions
- 2 crushed garlic cloves
- 1 tbsp tomato purée
- 200ml red wine
- 2 x 400g tins of chopped tomatoes
- ½ bunch of torn fresh basil

- 240g pack of peppered smoked mackerel fillets
- ½ bunch of basil
- 100ml light crème fraîche
- 50g grated mature cheddar

Preparation Instructions :

1. Oven temperature set to 200°C/180°C fan/gas 6. Pasta shells should be cooked for 2 minutes less than recommended on the package in a big pan of boiling water. During the last two minutes of cooking, add the head of broccoli, cut into florets, and then drain and leave aside.

2. Meanwhile, in a large sauté pan, heat a glug of oil and fry the red onions for 5 minutes. Add the garlic and tomato purée, fry for a few minutes, then add the red wine. Bubble for 2 minutes, then add the chopped tomatoes and basil. Cook for 10 minutes, then season.

3. The mackerel fillets should be skin-free and cut into bite-sized pieces. Stir into the pan with the remaining basil and light crème fraîche. Spoon into a 2 litre baking dish (or keep in the pan if it's ovenproof) and top with grated mature cheddar. Cook in the oven for 20-25 minutes until golden and piping hot throughout.

Nutritional Value Per Serving :

Calories: 688   fat: 29.7g
protein: 29.9g   carbs: 61.5g
Fibre : 8.6g   Sodium:1.4g

Mackerel and kale puff pastry tart

Prep time: 25 minutes
Cook time: 20-25 min
Serves 4

Ingredients

- 375g block of puff pastry

- Glug of olive oil
- 100g smoked bacon lardons
- 1 small finely chopped onion
- 80g kale
- 240g pack of peppered smoked mackerel fillets
- 200ml light crème fraîche
- 1 lemon

Preparation Instructions :

1. Heat the oven to 200°C/180°C fan/gas 6. Roll out the pastry to the thickness of a pound coin, then, using a plate as a guide, cut out a 20-23cm circle (keep the leftover pastry for another recipe). Slide onto a non-stick baking sheet and bake for 15-20 minutes until puffed, golden, and cooked through, then leave to cool on the sheet.

2. Meanwhile, heat a generous amount of olive oil in a nonstick pan and sauté the onion and smoked bacon lardons for 5 to 10 minutes. Add the kale, cook for 2 minutes until it wilts, then stir in the mackerel fillets, skin removed and flesh flaked, with a squeeze of lemon. Spread the light crème fraîche on the pastry, then spoon on the topping. Add a squeeze of lemon.

Nutritional Value Per Serving :

Calories: 688   fat: 29.7g
protein: 29.9g   carbs: 61.5g
Fibre : 8.6g   Sodium:1.4g

Cockles with leeks, Pernod, dill, and cream

Prep time: 25 minutes
Cook time: 20-25 min
Serves 4

Ingredients

- 1kg live cockles (or mussels, scrubbed and

de-bearded, if you can't find cockles)
- 1 medium leek
- 1 tbsp olive oil
- Small knob of butter
- 2 large garlic cloves, peeled
- 1 tsp fennel seeds, lightly crushed
- 20ml Pernod or other pastis mixed with 100ml water
- 100ml double cream
- 2 tbsp chopped fresh dill
- Lemon wedges and bread and butter to serve

You'll also need...
- Large heavy-based saucepan with a lid

Preparation Instructions :

1. Rinse the cockles well, discarding any broken or cracked shells. Clean them thoroughly to get rid of any sand or grit. Give the shells a gentle tap if they are open; if they don't close, throw them away.

2. Trim away the tough green part of the leek, trim back the root at its base, then slice the leek into 0.5-1cm rounds. Carefully wash the sliced leek in plenty of cold water, drain well and set aside.

3. Heat a large, heavy-based pan, then add the olive oil and butter. When it's foaming add the leek rounds. Fry gently for 4-5 minutes, shaking the pan and turning them occasionally. Add the garlic, crushed fennel, and a little salt and pepper, cook for another minute, then turn up the heat to high and add the cockles, the diluted Pernod, and the cream.

4. Put the lid on the pan and bring it up to a boil. Cook for 3-4 minutes or until the cockles are all open. A shuffle and a shake of the pan will encourage them to do so (discard any that remain closed).

5. Use a large slotted spoon to lift the cockles out of the pan and straight into 2 large warm serving bowls. Add the chopped dill to the simmering sauce in the pan and stir

well, then taste and adjust the seasoning if required.

6. Spoon the leeks, along with the lovely creamy dill and fennel seed sauce, over the cockles in the bowls and serve immediately with good bread and butter and wedges of lemon for squeezing over.

Nutritional Value Per Serving :

Calories: 525	fat: 40.5g
protein: 28.6g	carbs: 4.2g
Fibre : 3.6g	Sodium:1.1g

Crunchy-melty tuna and broccoli pasta bake

Prep time: 25 minutes
Cook time: 20-25 min
Serves 4

Ingredients
- 2 red onions, finely chopped
- 3 tbsp white wine vinegar
- 500g macaroni
- 300g tender stem broccoli, roughly chopped
- 1 tbsp olive oil, plus extra for drizzling
- 40g butter
- 40g plain flour
- 600ml semi-skimmed milk
- 1 tbsp dijon mustard
- 150g cheddar, grated
- 75g gruyère, grated
- 3 tbsp capers, drained
- 2 x 185g tins tuna in oil, drained and flaked
- Small bunch of fresh flat-leaf parsley, roughly chopped
- 2-3 slices stale sourdough bread, torn into chunky pieces

You'll also need...
- 2.5-liter ovenproof baking dish

Preparation Instructions :

1. Heat the oven to 200°C/180°C fan/gas 6.

Combine the minced onions and vinegar in a small bowl, then set it aside (this helps to mellow the flavor of the onion).

2. The pasta should be cooked for 2 minutes less than recommended on the package in a big pan of salted water that has been brought to a boil. Add the broccoli to the pasta pan 2 minutes before the end of the reduced cooking time. Both should be drained and returned to the pan. Add a little olive oil, mix, and then set the pan aside.

3. While the pasta is cooking, make the white sauce. Melt the butter in a large saucepan over medium heat. Add the flour and stir to make a roux, then cook for 1-2 minutes. Remove from the heat and gradually add the milk, stirring well after each addition to ensure there are no lumps. Return to the heat, bring to a boil, stirring constantly, then simmer for 2 minutes until thickened. Remove from the heat, stir in the dijon mustard, 100g cheddar, and 50g gruyère and allow to melt.

4. Add the drained pasta and broccoli, capers, tuna, and half of the parsley to the white sauce in the pan, along with the chopped onion that has been drained (remove the vinegar). Transfer to a large ovenproof dish then scatters over the remaining cheeses. Toss the sourdough chunks in 1 tbsp oil, then sprinkle over the top. Bake for 30 minutes until the croutons are golden and the bake is bubbling. Serve scattered with the remaining chopped parsley.

Nutritional Value Per Serving :

Calories: 578
fat: 21.9g
protein: 30.5g
carbs: 61.5g
Fibre : 6.1g
Sodium:1.3g

Hot-smoked salmon and asparagus tart

Prep time: 10 minutes
Cook time: 25 min
Serves 4

Ingredients
- 320g sheet of ready-rolled all-butter puff pastry
- 180g pack of full-fat cream cheese
- 4 tbsp good quality fresh pesto
- Pinch of sea salt flakes
- 100g fine asparagus spears
- Olive oil
- 100g peas
- 150g hot-smoked salmon
- Handful of watercress

Preparation Instructions :
1. Heat the oven to 200°C/180°C fan/gas 6. Unroll the puff pastry on its paper and put it on a baking tray. Spoon all of the cream cheese into a mixing bowl, stir a little to soften, then gently stir in the fresh pesto and a pinch of sea salt flakes until well marbled.

2. Brush the asparagus spears with a bit of olive oil. Using the tip of a small sharp knife, score a border 1.5cm from the edge of the pastry. Spread the cream cheese mixture inside the border. Top with the asparagus, and peas (defrosted if frozen) and bake on the middle shelf of the oven for 20 minutes until the edges of the tart are golden brown and puffed up.

3. Remove from the oven and flake over the hot-smoked salmon, then return to the oven to bake for a further 5 minutes. Top with a handful of watercress and drizzle over a little extra pesto to serve.

Nutritional Value Per Serving :
Calories: 602   fat: 43.4g
protein: 18.8g   carbs: 32g
Fibre : 4.2g   Sodium:2.1g

Tuna croquettes

Prep time: 25 minutes
Serves 8-10

Ingredients

- 2 baking potatoes
- 158g tin of drained and flaked tuna
- A handful of chopped fresh parsley, chopped
- Grated zest and juice of 1 lemon
- 1 free-range egg
- Plain flour, for dusting the croquettes
- 60g panko breadcrumbs
- Vegetable oil

Preparation Instructions :

1. To get the potatoes soft, prick them all over with a fork and microwave on high for 10 to 12 minutes. When the potatoes are cool, cut them in half and scoop the flesh into a basin, discarding the skins. (Or utilize the leftover 400g mash.)

2. Once the potato has been mashed with a knob of butter or splash of milk, add the canned tuna, fresh parsley, grated lemon zest, and egg yolk (save the white). Form into 8–10 croquettes, then lightly sprinkle with all-purpose flour. Beat the egg white in a bowl and put the panko breadcrumbs in a separate bowl. Dip each croquette in the egg, then coat in crumbs.

3. In a sauté pan, heat 1 cm of vegetable oil. Cook the croquettes in batches, flipping once, for 2 minutes, or until golden and crisp. Lemon wedges are optional.

Nutritional Value Per Serving :

Calories: 306
fat: 11.6g
protein: 13.8g
carbs: 35g
Fibre : 2.9g
Sodium:0.4g

Baked salmon gnocchi

Prep time: 15 minutes
Cook time: 12-14 min
Serves 4

Ingredients

- 2 tbsp olive oil
- 1 onion, finely sliced
- 1 large head of broccoli, separated into florets
- 300g reduced-fat cream cheese
- 3 tbsp pesto
- 400g fresh gnocchi
- Juice 1 lemon
- 4 small organic salmon fillets

Preparation Instructions :

1. Heat the oven to 200°C/180°C fan/gas 6. Heat the olive oil in a large ovenproof frying pan or shallow casserole and fry the onion for 2-3 minutes. Add the broccoli and stir-fry for a further 2 minutes.

2. Mix in the cream cheese, pesto, and 160ml water, then heat gently, stirring to combine. Meanwhile, microwave the gnocchi for 1 minute on high (or boil, following the pack instructions). Stir into the sauce with lots of black pepper, lemon juice, and salt to taste.

3. Place the gnocchi in a baking dish, add the salmon fillets to the sauce, and bake for 12 to 14 minutes, or until the fish is just cooked through. Serve immediately.

Nutritional Value Per Serving :

Calories: 618
fat: 34.2.6g
protein: 33.2g
carbs: 41.2g
Fibre : 5.9g
Sodium:2g

Pan-fried mackerel fillets with pear and pomegranate slaw

Prep time: 30 min
Serves 2

Ingredients

For the dressing
- 50ml soured cream
- 50ml good quality mayonnaise
- Juice and zest 1 lemon
- A bunch of fresh dills, finely chopped
- A bunch of fresh parsley, chopped
- 2 tsp sriracha sauce or other chili sauce

For the slaw
- 1 pear or apple, peeled, cored, and sliced
- ¼ red cabbage, shredded
- 100g pomegranate seeds
- Handful watercress leaves
- Handful blackberries (optional)
- For the mackerel

Olive oil for frying
- 2 slices sourdough, roughly torn
- 30g pine nuts, plus extra to serve
- Knob of unsalted butter
- 2 garlic cloves, bashed and peeled
- 3 bay leaves
- 2 whole mackerel, gutted, filleted, and pin-boned (ask your fishmonger to do this for you)

Preparation Instructions :

1. In a medium mixing bowl, combine all the ingredients for the dressing, saving half of the herbs. Mix thoroughly, then season to taste. Place aside.
2. For the slaw, put the pear/apple, cabbage, and half the pomegranate seeds in a serving bowl. Add the dressing and mix well.
3. For the mackerel, add a generous amount of oil to a big frying pan and heat it over medium heat. After seasoning and adding the pine nuts, add the sourdough and sauté it gently for a minute. The bread and pine nuts should both be faintly golden after a few more minutes of cooking. After that, remove from the pan and set aside.
4. Add the butter to the same pan with the bashed garlic cloves. Melt the butter and add the bay leaves. Leave the butter to foam for a few seconds, then add the mackerel fillets, skin-side down. Fry gently for 4-5 minutes, spooning the butter over. Carefully turn the fish over and cook for a further minute.
5. To serve, combine the slaw with sourdough, pine nuts, and some watercress. Serve the remaining herbs, watercress, pomegranate seeds, extra pine nuts, and a few blackberries, if desired, along with the fish.

Nutritional Value Per Serving :

Calories: 926	fat: 67.9g
protein: 33.4g	carbs: 40.4g
Fibre : 9.1g	Sodium:1.2g

The new fish and chips

Prep time: 20 min
Cook time : 35-40min
Serves 4

Ingredients
- 3 sweet potatoes, unpeeled (about 500g), sliced into thin wedges
- 400g parsnips, unpeeled, sliced into thin wedges
- Olive oil for roasting
- 50g fresh breadcrumbs
- 30g parmesan, grated
- 4 tbsp red pesto
- ½ bunch basil leaves chopped
- 4 x 150g sustainable cod loin fillets
- 3 tbsp mayonnaise
- Steamed peas to serve (optional)

Preparation Instructions :

1. Heat the oven to 200°C/180°C fan/gas 6. In a large roasting pan, combine the sweet potatoes and parsnips. Drizzle with olive oil and season with salt and pepper. Roast for 35 to 40 minutes, turning halfway through, until brown and crisp.

2. In a bowl, combine the parmesan and breadcrumbs. Combine half the red pesto and half the basil in another bowl. Spoon this over the fish, then top with the breadcrumbs and put on a baking tray.

3. When the wedges have 15 minutes of cooking time remaining, put the fish in the oven. Bake until golden on top and the flesh flakes easily.

4. Scatter the remaining basil on top of the fish. Stir the remaining pesto into the mayo and serve alongside the wedges and peas, if you like.

Nutritional Value Per Serving :

Calories: 560	fat: 23.4g
protein: 34.4g	carbs: 47.8g
Fibre : 9.2g	Sodium:1.1g

Beetroot-marinated salmon with dill pickled rice salad

Prep time: 30 min
Serves 6

Ingredients

- 4 organic skin-on salmon fillets
- 200g wild and basmati rice, rinsed
- 1 red onion, sliced
- Juice 1 lemon
- 50g dill pickles, chopped
- 1/2 x 25g pack of fresh dill, roughly chopped
- 1 whole raw beetroot (candy-striped), cut into matchsticks
- 2 tbsp extra-virgin olive oil
- Light olive oil for frying
- Fresh salad leaves to serve (optional)
- Crème fraîche to serve
- For the marinade
- 2 whole beetroot, grated
- 1 tbsp freshly grated horseradish
- Zest and juice 1 lemon, plus extra zest and juice to serve
- 1/2 x 25g pack of fresh dill, chopped
- 1 tbsp dijon mustard
- 3 tbsp extra-virgin olive oil
- Freshly milled black pepper

Preparation Instructions :

1. Put all the marinade ingredients in a bowl and mix well, then spoon half into a large food bag with the salmon fillets. Turn to coat, then leave in the refrigerator for an hour to marinate (or overnight if you like. To serve with the fish, cover and refrigerate the remaining marinade.

2. Boil the rice in 400ml water for 12-15 minutes until cooked but still with some bite. Drain, then thoroughly cool by rinsing under cold running water. In the meantime, combine the onion with a generous amount of salt, lemon juice, and a bowl and set aside for a few minutes.

3. Mix the cold rice with the dill pickles, fresh dill, beetroot matchsticks, extra-virgin olive oil, and red onion. Taste and season.

4. Heat a frying pan with a little oil, then fry the salmon, skin-side down, for 3-4 minutes until the skin is crisp. Carefully turn and cook for a minute or until cooked to your liking.

5. Serve the salmon with the rice salad, leaves (if using), and the rest of the marinade along with a dollop of crème fraîche and extra lemon zest and juice.

Nutritional Value Per Serving :

Calories: 696	fat: 37.1g
protein: 38.7g	carbs: 49g
Fibre : 5.6g	Sodium:0.8g

Beef stew

Prep time: 35 min:
Cook time 4-5 hours
Serves 4-6

Ingredients

- Olive oil for frying
- 3 small onions, each cut into 8 wedges
- 4 carrots, sliced into thick rounds
- 2 celery sticks, roughly sliced
- 200g chestnut mushrooms, halved
- 3 garlic cloves, sliced
- 1.5kg British braising steak, cut into chunky pieces
- 4 tbsp plain flour
- 1 tsp English mustard powder
- 4 tbsp tomato purée
- 330ml brown ale
- 4 Oxo beef stock cubes, dissolved in 800ml boiling water
- ½ tbsp Worcestershire sauce
- 4 bay leaves
- Seasonal potatoes to serve

Preparation Instructions :

1. Oven temperature set at 140°C/120°C fan/ gas 1. Heat a glug of oil in a casserole (one with a lid) over medium heat. Add the onions, carrots, and celery and fry for 8-10 minutes until softened. Stirring regularly, add the mushrooms, and cook for a further 4 minutes with the garlic.

2. In the meantime, preheat a frying pan with a generous amount of oil. In a bowl, toss the beef with the flour, mustard powder, and salt and pepper. Brown the beef in 2-3 batches, then add to the casserole with the tomato purée and ale. Stir well and bubble over high heat for 2-3 minutes. Pour in the stock and Worcestershire sauce and add the bay leaves. Bring to a boil, cover, put in the oven, and cook for 4½-5 hours.

3. Check the beef is tender (it should fall apart easily when prodded with a fork) taste and season with salt and pepper. Serve with seasonal potatoes.

Nutritional Value Per Serving :

Calories: 503	fat: 18.8g
protein: 58.7g	carbs: 19.8g
Fibre : 4.4g	Sodium:1.8g

Crumbed breast of lamb with watercress and Roquefort salad

Prep time: 50 min
Cook time: 2 HOURS 10-40 MIN, PLUS OVERNIGHT PRESSING
Serves 4

Ingredients

- 2 British lamb breasts, boned (ask for the bones)
- Vegetable oil for frying
- 2 onions, sliced
- 2 carrots, sliced
- 1 garlic bulb, halved horizontally
- A few fresh thyme sprigs
- A few fresh rosemary sprigs
- 200ml dry white wine
- 1-litre fresh chicken stock
- 4 tbsp dijon mustard
- 4-6 tbsp panko breadcrumbs
- Olive oil for drizzling
- For the salad

- 150g watercress
- 2 shallots, sliced into rings
- 1 red chili, deseeded and sliced
- 3 tbsp red wine vinegar
- Olive oil for drizzling
- 150g roquefort cheese

You'll also need...
- Large, flameproof lidded casserole

Preparation Instructions :

1. Heat the oven to 160°C/140°C fan/gas 3. Each lamb breast should be spread out before being divided into 4 smaller pieces. Good seasoning One piece of the lamb at a time, brown it all over in a hot skillet with a little oil, and then remove it.

2. The vegetables, garlic, and herbs should be added to the pan and cooked for 10 minutes at medium heat to soften. White wine should be added and simmered for two minutes. Add the stock, lamb, and lamb bones (if using) to the casserole. Cover with water.

3. Bring to a simmer, then cover the casserole with the lid and transfer to the oven to cook for 1½-2 hours until the lamb is tender.

4. After being cooked, gently remove the lamb from the cooking liquid and place it skin-up on a baking sheet covered with parchment paper. Another tray should be placed on top and covered with a second sheet of baking paper. Press the meat as it cools by using tins or a heavy pan as weights. Once cool, transfer to the fridge and press overnight.

5. Heat the oven to 180°C/160°C fan/gas 4. Slice each lamb piece in half again into 2 smaller fillets (you'll have 8 lamb pieces in total). Put each piece flat on a roasting tray, skin-side up, brush well with dijon mustard, then sprinkle over the breadcrumbs. Drizzle with a little olive

oil, then bake for 40 minutes until golden brown.

6. While the lamb is cooking, prepare the salad. Cut most of the thick stalks from the watercress bunch and put the leaves in a bowl. Add the shallots, chili and vinegar with a pinch of salt. Drizzle over a little olive oil, mix the salad gently, then crumble the Roquefort cheese over the top.

Nutritional Value Per Serving :

Calories: 969	fat: 59.9g
protein: 71.1g	carbs: 24.5g
Fibre : 5.8g	Sodium:4g

Roast pork belly with figs, pears, and sherry

Prep time: 20 min
Cook time : 4-4½ hours, plus overnight chilling
Serves 6-8

Ingredients
- 1.5kg British free-range pork belly, on the bone, skin scored
- 2 tsp caraway seeds
- Large pinch-dried chili flakes
- A few thyme sprig leaves picked
- 1 tsp sea salt flakes
- 2 onions, peeled and quartered
- 1 large leek or 2 carrots, cut into chunks
- 300ml dry sherry (such as fino or amontillado)
- 4 ripe figs, halved
- 2 pears, quartered and cored

You'll also need...

Pestle and mortar

Preparation Instructions :

1. The night before cooking, unwrap the pork, put it on a lidded plate or tray, and cover it with a tea towel. Put them at the

bottom of the fridge, well away from food that will be eaten raw, until you are ready to cook.

2. Heat the oven to 220°C/200°C fan/gas 7. Remove the pork from the fridge 30 minutes before cooking to take the chill off it. Pat the skin dry with kitchen paper. Grind the spices and thyme leaves in a pestle and mortar, add a good grind of black pepper, then rub the mixture into the pork meat. Rub the salt into the skin, then put the meat in a snug-fitting, heavy-based roasting tin, skin-side up. Put the tin in the oven and roast for 45 minutes, or until the skin crackles.

3. Remove the tin, turn down the oven to 170°C/150°C fan/gas 3½, then transfer the pork to a board. Put the onions, leeks, and carrots in the tin to form a trivet, then sit the pork on top and add the sherry and 100 ml cold water. Return the pork to the oven for 3 hours, checking every hour or so and adding a little extra water if it starts to dry out. After 3 hours, wiggle one of the bones. If it feels loose enough to come away easily from the flesh, remove the pork from the oven. If not, cook for 20-30 minutes more.

4. Once the pork is tender, remove the tin from the oven and add the figs and pears, turning them to coat them in the cooking juices. Turn up the oven to 200°C/180°C fan/gas 6, then return the pork for 10-15 minutes. If the skin is crisp, remove the tin from the oven and rest the meat on a warm plate for 20 minutes. If it's not fully crackled, cook the pork for another 20 minutes or until the skin is crisp.

5. When you're ready to serve, put the pork skin-side down on a chopping board, pull out the bones, then carve into generous slices.

6. Put the pork, fig halves, and pear quarters on a platter, then spoon over the cooking juices from the tin. Serve with potatoes and any steamed vegetables you fancy.

Nutritional Value Per Serving :

Calories: 581	fat: 38.3g
protein: 37.3g	carbs: 10g
Fibre : 2.9g	Sodium:1g

Slow-roast pork belly with lemon, parsley, and caper gremolata

Prep time: 30 min
Cook time: 4 hours and 10 min
Serves 6

Ingredients

- 2kg piece British free-range pork belly, boneless (ask your butcher to remove, score and reserve the pork belly skin for you in a single piece)
- Knob of butter, softened
- 2 tbsp chopped fresh sage
- 1 tsp fennel seeds, toasted and lightly ground in a pestle and mortar
- 300ml good quality chicken stock
- 300ml dry white wine
- 2 tbsp olive oil
- 4 tbsp capers, rinsed and dried
- Finely grated zest 2 lemons
- 1 garlic clove, finely chopped
- 4 tbsp roughly chopped fresh parsley
- Baby carrots to serve (optional)

You'll also need...

- Roomy roasting tin; kitchen string; kitchen scissors; baking tray lined with compostable baking paper

Preparation Instructions :

1. Heat the oven to 220°C/200°C fan/gas 7. Lay the pork belly flat on a work surface. Mix the softened butter, sage, fennel, a little salt, and a grinding of black

pepper. Rub the mixture all over the pork, spreading it thinly. Roll up the belly in a cylinder shape, put the skin back on top to cover the whole joint, and then use kitchen string to tie the skin firmly in place at 2cm intervals, tying it securely. Put the pork aside in the roasting tin.

2. Pour the stock and wine around the meat, then transfer it to the oven and roast for 20 minutes. After 20 minutes, wrap the whole roasting tin loosely in foil, turn down the oven temperature to 150°C/130°C fan/gas 2 and return the tin to the oven to roast for a further 3½ hours.

3. Meanwhile, heat the olive oil in a small frying pan until hot. Add the capers and fry for 2-3 minutes, until crisp and golden. Remove the pan from the oven. Set the capers aside.

4. After 3½ hours, remove the pork from the oven. Increase the temperature to 220°C/200°C fan/gas 7. Snip the string holding the pork skin and transfer the roast to a board (be careful, as it will be very hot). Wrap the pork belly in foil and set aside to rest for 20 minutes. Meanwhile, pour the pork juices into a small saucepan.

5. Using kitchen scissors, cut the pork skin into thin strips. Arrange on the lined baking tray, then roast in the oven for 20 minutes more, or until the skin is beautifully crisp and golden.

6. Meanwhile, spoon off and discard the layer of fat sitting on top of the juices in the saucepan. Set the pan over medium heat, bring to a boil, and simmer for 10 minutes or until slightly reduced. Take off the heat and keep warm.

7. In a small bowl, combine the crispy capers, lemon zest, garlic, and parsley to make the gremolata. Carve the pork into slices, then arrange it on warmed plates. Top with the gremolata and strips of crispy crackling,

then serve with the Hasselback potatoes and caramelized apples, plus steamed carrots if you like, all drizzled with the gravy.

Nutritional Value Per Serving :

Calories: 581	fat: 38.3g
protein: 37.3g	carbs: 10g
Fibre : 2.9g	Sodium:1g

James Martin's stuffed leg of Welsh lamb with onion and leek sauce

Prep time: 25 min
Cook time: 1 hour and 30 min
Serves 6

Ingredients

- 2kg Welsh lamb leg, boned
- For the stuffing
- Small bunch of fresh flatleaf parsley, chopped
- ½ small bunch of fresh mint, chopped
- 4 garlic cloves, finely chopped
- 150g breadcrumbs
- 1 tbsp dijon mustard
- 50g hazelnuts, roughly chopped
- 1 medium free-range egg
- 150g black pudding, chopped
- For the sauce
- 25g salted butter
- 1 large onion, chopped
- 2 leeks, chopped
- 1 heaped tbsp plain flour
- 25ml dry white wine
- 400ml whole milk
- 100ml double cream
- 2-3 flatleaf parsley sprigs, chopped

You'll also need...
- Cook's string

Preparation Instructions :

1. Heat the oven to 240°C/220°C fan/gas 9.

Put the lamb skin-side down on a board, then open it out and season.

2. Use a food processor to finely chop the parsley and mint for the stuffing. Add the hazelnuts, egg, mustard, breadcrumbs, and garlic. Season and blend once more to mix (or chop everything finely for coarse stuffing).

3. Spread the stuffing all over the inside of the boned lamb, then scatter over the black pudding, and season again. Roll up the lamb to enclose the stuffing, then tie it securely with string along the length of the stuffed joint. Put on a rack in a large roasting tin and roast for 30 minutes, then reduce the temperature to 200°C/180°C fan/gas 6 and roast for a further 1 hour. Set aside the bowl to rest for 30 minutes.

4. In the meantime, melt the butter in a skillet over medium heat to prepare the sauce. Add the onion when it has melted and begun to bubble, then simmer it for 5 minutes while stirring frequently. Cook for another 2 minutes after adding the leeks. For 30 to 60 seconds, add the flour after stirring. season, whisk in the milk, cream, and wine, then season once more before incorporating the parsley.

5. Lift the lamb onto a board, then untie the lamb. Slice and serve with the sauce, any resting juices, roast potatoes, and seasonal greens.

Nutritional Value Per Serving :

Calories: 675	fat: 38.3g
protein: 36.7g	carbs: 25.3g
Fibre : 3.5g	Sodium:1.2g

Slow-roast pork shoulder with leeks and cannellini beans

Prep time: 25 min

Cook time: 4 hours and 50 min
Serves 6

Ingredients

- 2 tsp fennel seeds
- Finely grated zest 1 orange
- 5-6 garlic cloves, peeled and bashed
- 5 tbsp olive oil, plus extra to drizzle
- 1.8kg British outdoor-bred boneless, rolled pork shoulder, skin on, scored at 12mm intervals (ask your butcher to score the skin)
- 3 leeks, trimmed, finely sliced, and rinsed
- 2 fennel bulbs, trimmed and sliced into thin wedges
- 2 bay leaves
- 175ml dry white wine
- 1 tbsp English mustard
- 2 x 400g tins cannellini beans (undrained)
- 300ml chicken stock (make sure it's gluten-free if it needs to be)
- Splash cider vinegar

You'll also need…

- Large, wide, hob-safe casserole or heavy roasting tray

Preparation Instructions :

1. In a pestle and mortar, combine the fennel seeds with a generous quantity of salt and pepper, and grind to a fine powder. Crush once more after adding the orange zest and two of the crushed garlic cloves. Add a few tablespoons of olive oil and combine. Rub the pork with this mixture.

2. The oven should be preheated to 230°C/210°C fan/gas 8 when you are ready to cook the meat. Pour two tablespoons of olive oil into the casserole or roasting pan and place over low heat. Leeks and the remaining garlic are added, and they are cooked on the stove for about 10 minutes, or until they begin to soften.

3. Bring the wine and mustard to a boil, then reduce it by half after adding the fennel, bay leaves, and wine. Bring back to a boil

after stirring in the liquid from the beans and the chicken stock.

4. Place the pork that has been marinated on top of the beans, gently pressing it in, and brush the skin with a little oil. To allow the skin time to crisp up and crackle, roast for 30 minutes. Take out of the oven, then tightly wrap in foil or a lid. Return the casserole or tray to the oven, reduce the temperature to 160°C/140°C fan/gas 3, and cook the food for another 3 to 4 hours, or until the meat is soft and falling apart.

5. Turn the oven back up to 230°C/210°C fan/gas 8 and remove the cover or foil. The crackling will get crisp again as a result, but watch it carefully and take the roast out of the oven after about 20 minutes. Before serving, trim off any extra fat from the beans and give them a final spritz of cider vinegar.

Nutritional Value Per Serving :

Calories: 630
fat: 24.5g
protein: 74.1g
carbs: 17.8g
Fibre : 10.3g
Sodium:0.5g

Steak with anchovy and caper butter

Prep time: 15 min
Serves 1

Ingredients

- Vegetable oil
- 250g British rib-eye steak
- Large knob of butter
- 2 chopped anchovy fillets
- 2 tbsp drained capers
- To serve: chips, watercress, and mustard

Preparation Instructions :

1. In a hot pan, heat a small amount of vegetable oil. Salt and pepper the meat before placing it in the heated pan. Cook the meat (for medium-rare) for 2 to 3 minutes on each side, or until the outside is brown and beginning to crisp at the edges. Then, place the meat on a warm dish to rest.

2. Put a large knob of butter, the chopped anchovy fillets, and the capers back on the fire. Stir to heat through and remove any browned bits from the pan's bottom.

3. Return the steak to the pan along with any resting juices and spoon the hot butter over to coat. Top with a knob of fresh butter and serve with chips, watercress, and your favorite mustard.

Nutritional Value Per Serving :

Calories: 681
fat: 23.2G SATURATED
protein: 62.1g
carbs: 1g
Fibre: 1.2g
Sodium:1.6g

Sticky ribs in rhubarb, ginger, and chili

Prep time: 30 min
Cook time: 2-3 hours
Serves 6

Ingredients

- About 2kg organic pork ribs, cut into 2-3 rib sections
- 225g rhubarb (about 2 large stalks)
- 1 large thumb-size piece of fresh ginger, finely grated
- 4 garlic cloves, thinly sliced
- 2 fresh red chilies, halved, deseeded, and thinly sliced

- 1 tbsp coriander seeds, toasted briefly in a dry pan, then crushed
- 3 tbsp soft brown sugar
- 4 tbsp soy sauce
- 125ml apple juice
- 1 tbsp sesame seeds

Preparation Instructions :

1. Oven temperature set at 140°C/120°C fan/gas 1. If you can, arrange the ribs in a single layer in a large roasting pan. Salt and pepper the ribs and add a small glass of water (approximately 175ml) to the dish. Cover the ribs with some baking paper before covering the entire dish with foil. Make sure the sides are sealed snugly to prevent steam leakage. Put the tray in the oven and cook for 2-2½ hours.

2. Meanwhile, make the sauce. Slice the rhubarb into 0.5cm pieces and put them in a bowl with the ginger, garlic, chilies, crushed coriander seeds, sugar, soy sauce, apple juice, and sesame seeds. Mix well.

3. Remove the ribs from the oven, then take the foil and baking paper off the dish—the rib meat should be lovely and tender by now. Increase the oven temperature to 190°C/170°C fan/gas 5.

4. Spoon the sauce over the ribs, making sure you coat them, then put the dish back in the oven, uncovered, and bake for 30 to 40 minutes. The sauce will begin to thicken as the rhubarb breaks up and the apple juice reduces. Check the ribs every 10–15 minutes, spooning over the sauce as it thickens. When it's rich and sticky, remove the ribs from the oven and leave them to rest for 10–15 minutes before serving.

Nutritional Value Per Serving :

Calories: 340
fat: 18G
protein: 31.8g

carbs: 12g
Fibre : 1.2g
Sodium:1.6g

Rack of lamb, potato, and pepper tray roast

Prep time: 20 min
Cook time: 1 hour
Serves 4

Ingredients

- 750g small new potatoes, roughly sliced
- 3 mixed romano peppers (or regular peppers), roughly cut into chunks
- 2 red onions, thickly sliced
- 3 tbsp olive oil
- 1 rack of lamb, trimmed (choose one with 8 ribs)
- 2 tbsp dijon mustard
- Handful each chopped fresh flatleaf parsley and coriander
- Finely grated zest 1 lemon, plus the lemon, quartered to serve
- 1 chunky slice of crusty bread, whizzed/grated to make breadcrumbs
- 200g tender stem broccoli, any large spears halved
- 6-8 tbsp natural yogurt
- 50g smoked salted almonds, roughly chopped (you can use plain almonds if you can't get smoked almonds)

Preparation Instructions :

1. Set the oven's temperature to 220°C/200°C fan/gas 7. In a large shallow roasting pan, combine the potatoes, peppers, and onions with 2 tablespoons of the oil and a generous pinch of salt and pepper. For 30 minutes, roast.

2. Meanwhile prepare the lamb rack. In a small bowl mix the dijon mustard, half the chopped herbs, and the lemon zest with

salt and pepper. Coat the lamb with the mustard mix, then pat the breadcrumbs over the top to coat.

3. After taking the roasting pan out of the oven, add the broccoli and toss everything together. The remaining oil should be drizzled over the lamb, and it should roast for 25 to 30 minutes from medium-rare to medium (or 5 minutes longer if you prefer your meat more well done).

4. Set aside the rack of lamb for 10 minutes of resting. In the meantime, combine everything in the tray, sprinkle with yogurt, and top with almonds and the chopped herbs you'd like to save. Slice the rested lamb into individual ribs, and place them on a plate at the table so that guests can assist themselves.

Nutritional Value Per Serving :

Calories: 686
fat: 31.6g
protein: 48.1g
carbs: 55.8g
Fibre : 10.8g
Sodium:1.3g

Mustard, honey, and lime pork chops with apple slaw

Prep time: 35 min Plus marinating and resting
Serves 4

Ingredients

- 4 thick outdoor-reared British pork chops on the bone (around 300g each)
- 2 tbsp white wine vinegar
- 2 tbsp soft light brown sugar
- 1 tbsp sea salt
- 1/2 tbsp cracked black pepper
- 2 tbsp mixed chopped fresh parsley, chives, and tarragon
- 1 kg small to medium waxy potatoes, such as charlotte
- 2 tbsp olive oil
- For the dressing
- 100ml extra-virgin olive oil
- 1 tbsp wholegrain mustard
- 1 tbsp runny honey
- Finely grated zest and juice 1/2 lime
- 1 tbsp chopped fresh coriander
- For the slaw
- 1 tsp fennel seeds
- 1/4-1/2 green cabbage, core removed, leaves shredded
- 1 small onion, very thinly sliced
- 1 apple, cored, quartered, and cut into thin batons
- 2 tsp lime juice
- 1/4 tsp each of sugar and sea salt
- 4 tbsp soured cream (optional)

You'll also need
- Pestle and mortar or spice grinder

Preparation Instructions :

1. Put the pork chops in a shallow container. Mix 1 litre cold water with the vinegar, sugar, salt, and black pepper, then pour over the chops. Cover and chill overnight. The next day, remove the chops from the brine and pat dry. Put them on a rack over a plate and chill for 4 hours if possible.

2. Olive oil, mustard, honey, lime zest, 2 tsp of lime juice (save the rest), coriander, salt, and pepper should all be combined in a jar to make the dressing. Shake the sealed container to ensure even mixing, then save until needed.

3. Make the slaw next by toasting the fennel seeds for 3–4 minutes over medium heat, or until they become golden and release a delicious aroma. After cooling, coarsely ground the spices in a spice grinder or pestle and mortar. In a container, mix the fennel seeds, apple, cabbage, and onion. Stir in the remaining dressing-related lime

juice, sugar, salt, and some pepper. Add the soured cream right before serving, if using, and chill until needed.

4. When the chops are ready to cook, place them on a rack over an open flame or barbeque grill, and sear them for 2-3 minutes on each side, or until golden. Cook the chops for 5–6 minutes, then move them to a cooler part of the fire or barbecue or raise the rack higher. Once removed, dress with dressing. Serve with the slaw after resting for five minutes while loosely wrapped in foil.

Nutritional Value Per Serving :

Calories: 636
fat: 34.1g
protein: 68g
carbs: 12.7g
Fibre : 3.2g
Sodium:1.4g

Lamb shank hotpot pie with pickled red cabbage

Prep time: 35 min
Cook time 30-40 min 2 hours to 30 min + cooling overnight pickling
Serves 6

Ingredients

- 50g plain flour, plus extra to dust
- 6 organic lamb shanks (about 350g each)
- 2 tbsp olive oil
- 2 medium onions, cut into wedges
- 3 carrots, chopped
- 2 large potatoes, diced
- 2 garlic cloves, crushed
- 2 tbsp finely chopped fresh rosemary leaves
- 1.2 liters lamb or chicken stock
- 320g ready-rolled puff pastry
- 1 medium free-range egg, lightly beaten, to glaze

- For the pickled red cabbage
- 500g red cabbage, core removed, leaves finely shredded
- 1 red onion, finely sliced
- 200ml red wine vinegar
- 1 tbsp caster sugar

You'll also need

- Large saucepan or flameproof casserole
- 2.5-3 liter pie dish

Preparation Instructions :

1. To make the pickled cabbage: put the red cabbage in a large heatproof non-reactive bowl. Put the onion, vinegar, and sugar in a small stainless steel saucepan over high heat and boil for about 10 minutes until the onion starts to soften. Pour the mixture over the cabbage, stir well, then leave to cool completely. Cover and chill to pickle overnight or until needed.

2. Add the lamb shanks to the flour after seasoning it with salt and pepper for the pie. The shanks should be thoroughly browned after the skillet or dish has heated up. The potatoes, onions, carrots, and rosemary should all be added to the pan or casserole, along with any leftover seasoned flour. Stir well. Pour the stock over the meat, topping it with a little water if necessary. Once the mixture has come to a boil, cover it and cook it very gently for two hours, or until the meat falls from the bone. Take the meat out of the skillet. After shredding the flesh, set aside 3 of the bones. If necessary, reduce the cooking liquid by bubbling it over medium heat to around 2 liters.

3. Heat the oven to 200°C/180°C fan/gas 6. Transfer the lamb and liquid to the pie dish, putting the reserved lamb bones on top in a line down the center, then leave to cool.

4. Roll out the pastry on a lightly floured

surface until it is 4mm thick and large enough to cover the pie. Brush the rim of the dish with a little beaten egg, then cut 3 slits in the rolled-out pastry to match the bones. Lay the pastry lid over the top, sliding the bones through the slits. Press down the edges of the pastry to seal, then trim off any excess pastry and crimp the edges with your fingers or a fork. Brush with beaten egg to glaze.

5. Bake the pie for 30–40 minutes, until the pastry is puffed and golden and the filling is bubbling. Serve with the pickled red cabbage alongside.

Nutritional Value Per Serving :

Calories: 731
fat: 35.9g
protein: 39g
carbs: 57.1g
Fibre : 9.5g
Sodium:1g

Crab apple and chili glazed beef sirloin

Prep time: 25 min
Cook time 40 min + coolingand resting
Serves 6

Ingredients

- 35g anchovy fillets in oil, drained and finely chopped
- 2 tsp sherry vinegar
- 120g crab apple jelly
- ½-2 tsp chili flakes or crushed pink peppercorns to taste
- 1 tbsp olive oil or beef dripping
- 1.2kg boneless British beef sirloin, lightly seasoned with salt and pepper (at room temperature)
- For the watercress crème
- 300g crème fraîche

- 1 large garlic clove, crushed
- ½ tsp sea salt
- 2 tsp sherry vinegar
- Squeeze lemon juice (optional)
- 3 tbsp good quality extra virgin olive oil
- Large handful of watercress, very finely chopped, plus extra leaves to serve

You'll also need

- Flameproof roasting tin
- Useful to have
- Digital probe thermometer

Preparation Instructions :

1. The anchovy fillets should be thoroughly blended with the vinegar before adding the jelly, chili flakes, or pink peppercorns to create the glaze. Place aside.

2. Over medium-high heat, place a roasting pan. After 30 seconds, put the sirloin, fat side down, into the tin with the oil or dripping. The meat should be browned for about 5 minutes, until golden, before being turned and browned for about 3 minutes on each side. Remove the meat from the fire, coat it with two-thirds of the glaze, cover it with foil, and let it cool to room temperature.

3. Heat the oven to 200°C/180°C fan/gas 6, remove the foil from the meat (keep it handy), and roast for 25 minutes. Turn the oven down to 180°C/160°C fan/gas 4, remove the meat from the oven, and brush with the remaining glaze. Cover loosely with foil, then return to the oven for a further 10-20 minutes, depending on how thick the joint is and how you like it cooked. If you have a probe thermometer it should be 50°C in the middle for rare, 55°C for medium-rare, and 60°C for medium (the temperature in the center will rise by about five degrees as it rests). Once cooked to your liking, remove from the oven and leave the meat to rest on a lipped board or tray for 10 minutes, loosely

covered in foil, then slice to serve.

4. Make the watercress crème in the meantime. Mix the crème fraîche, garlic, salt, vinegar, lemon juice, and extra virgin olive oil with a balloon whisk until thoroughly combined. Then taste and adjust the seasoning, adding more salt or lemon juice as needed. Stir in the chopped watercress. Place the watercress leaves around the beef in the serving dish, then pour any remaining glaze or liquids from the roasting pan over it. Serve alongside the roast potatoes, seasonal greens, and watercress crème.

5. Bake the pie for 30–40 minutes, until the pastry is puffed and golden and the filling is bubbling. Serve with the pickled red cabbage alongside.

Nutritional Value Per Serving :

Calories: 860	fat: 73.6g
protein: 36g	carbs: 13.4g
Fibre : 0.1g	Sodium:1.6g

Barbecued rack of mutton with broad beans, peas, and lovage

Prep time: 45 min
Serves 4

Ingredients

- 1 rack of mutton (700-800g), trimmed
- 2 garlic cloves, grated
- Grated zest 1 lemon
- 1 tbsp fennel seeds, crushed
- Good pinch chili flakes
- 2 tbsp chopped fresh lovage (or fresh parsley if you can't find lovage)
- 4 tbsp olive oil
- 250g broad beans (podded weight)
- 250g fresh peas (or use frozen)

You'll also need...

- Digital probe thermometer
- Barbecue (charcoal or gas)

Preparation Instructions :

1. Place the rack of mutton fat-side up on a work surface. Cut the fat in a crisscross pattern with the tip of a sharp knife, almost to the level of the meat.

2. In a bowl, combine the olive oil, garlic, lemon zest, fennel seeds, chili flakes, lovage or parsley, and a little salt and pepper. Make sure to cover the mutton completely with the remaining half of this herbaceous marinade. Cover and set aside to marinate for a few hours if you can. Reserve the remaining marinade.

3. If cooking on a charcoal barbecue light it an hour before you plan to cook the mutton.

4. Bring to a boil some salted water in a pan. Add the broad beans and boil for about a minute. Next, add the peas and simmer for approximately four minutes, or until the peas are fully cooked. Good drainage

5. Warm a frying pan over medium-high heat. Add the reserved marinade and, when it's sizzling, add the drained broad beans and peas along with plenty of salt and pepper. Toss everything together to coat, then remove from the heat and keep warm.

6. Put the mutton rack bone-side down on a medium-hot barbecue grill and cook over direct heat for 12-15 minutes. Turn the mutton rack over and cook the other side for a further 12-15 minutes, checking it regularly. If at any point the meat seems to be coloring too much or the fire flares up, remove it and allow the flames to die back a little before putting it back over the heat. When the center of the joint reaches 55°C when tested with the thermometer, remove the mutton from the heat. Put on top of the peas and broad beans and leave to rest for 10 minutes, then carve and serve.

Nutritional Value Per Serving :

Calories: 448

fat: 25.3g

protein: 39.1g

carbs: 11.4g

Fibre : 9.1g

Sodium:0.3g

Creamy mushroom and chestnut pork with apple

Prep time: 45 min

Cook time: 40 min

Serves 4

Ingredients

- Olive oil for frying
- 4 thick 250g British outdoor-reared pork chops on the bone
- 100ml brandy
- 100g butter
- 1 red onion, cut into thick slices
- 1 red apple, cut into thick slices
- 200g button mushrooms
- 1 onion, finely chopped
- 2 celery sticks, finely chopped
- 2 garlic cloves, sliced
- 1 bay leaf
- 4 fresh thyme sprigs
- 250ml chicken stock
- 200g cooked, peeled vacuum-packed chestnuts, chopped
- Nutmeg for grating
- 200ml double cream
- 30g dried wild mushrooms, soaked in 200ml boiling water
- 6 fresh sage leaves

You'll also need...

- 2-liter baking dish

Preparation Instructions :

1. Heat the oil in a frying pan. The pork chops are seasoned, cooked for 3–4 minutes until golden on each side, and then transferred to a platter. After turning off the heat, add the brandy while using a wooden spoon to scrape the pan's bottom. Put some in a bowl.

2. Add half the butter and bring the heat back to medium. With a bit of salt, cook the red onion, apple, and button mushrooms for 5 to 6 minutes, or until they are caramelized, and then put aside.

3. Meanwhile, melt the remaining 50g butter in a medium saucepan and cook the onion, celery, garlic, bay leaf, thyme sprigs, and a pinch of salt for 10 minutes or until soft.

4. Add the brandy that was set aside, then simmer for 5 minutes, or until syrupy. Add half of the chestnuts and the stock. After bringing it to a boil, reduce the heat, cover it it, and simmer for 20 minutes.

5. After removing the thyme and bay leaf, puree the sauce in a stick blender until it is smooth. Add a few nutmeg gratings, salt, and pepper to taste, and then mix in the cream.

6. Heat the oven to 190°C/170°C fan/gas 5. Arrange the pork, onion, apple, and mushrooms in the baking dish. Strain the dried mushrooms through a fine sieve into the sauce, then stir. Add the mushrooms, discarding any grit. Pour the sauce over the pork, scatter over the remaining chestnuts and sage, then bake, covered with foil, for 30 minutes. Uncover and bake for 10 minutes to brown.

Nutritional Value Per Serving :

Calories: 1008

fat: 65.1g

protein: 60.4g

carbs: 28g

Fibre : 6.5g

Sodium:1.1g

Whole baked cauliflower with pearl barley, wild mushrooms and cheese

Prep time: 1 hour
Cook time: 30-35 min
Serves 4

Ingredients

- 1 large cauliflower (about 800g), leaves removed and reserved (chopped if large)
- Olive oil for frying
- 1 onion, finely sliced
- 2 leeks, finely sliced
- 2 garlic cloves, crushed
- 4 fresh thyme sprigs
- 180g pearl barley
- 300ml dry white wine
- 1.2 litres vegetable stock
- 250ml single cream
- Juice 1 lemon
- 200g wild mushrooms, such as girolle and oyster
- 100g lincolnshire poacher or mature cheddar
- Truffle oil to drizzle (optional)

You'll also need...

- Shallow flameproof casserole

Preparation Instructions :

1. Heat the oven to 220°C/200°C fan/gas 7. The whole cauliflower should be cooked in a big pan of boiling water for 10 minutes, or until it is almost soft. Drain, rinse with cold water, then repeat with a second drain and a kitchen towel to dry.

2. Heat a glug of oil in the casserole, add the onion and leeks, and fry gently for 10 minutes until softened.

3. Add the garlic, thyme sprigs, and pearl barley, then fry for a few minutes. Turn up the heat, add the wine, and bubble to reduce for 5 minutes, then add the stock and simmer for 20-25 minutes until the barley is nearly tender, stirring occasionally with a wooden spoon. Stir in the cream, the reserved cauliflower leaves, and the lemon juice, then simmer for another 5 minutes.

4. Meanwhile, in a non-stick frying pan, heat a glug of oil over a high heat and fry the mushrooms for 5 minutes, until they start to colour and are starting to soften. Add them to the sauce, taste and season.

5. Sit the cauliflower on top of the sauce. Grate over the cheese, then bake in the oven for 30-35 minutes until golden and bubbling. To serve, drizzle over a little truffle oil, if you like.

Nutritional Value Per Serving :

Calories: 627	fat: 28.7g
protein: 21g	carbs: 53.5g
Fibre : 8.2g	Sodium:0.6g

Jersey royal, onion, sherry and tarragon bake

Prep time: 20 min
Cook time: 25 min
Serves 4-6

Ingredients

- Butter, for greasing
- 1kg jersey royal potatoes
- 4 large onions and chop

- A small bunch of fresh tarragon
- 3 garlic cloves,
- 100ml fino sherry
- 40ml double cream
- 50g gruyère or vegetarian alternative
- 40g fresh breadcrumbs

Preparation Instructions :

1. Set the oven's temperature to 220°C/fan200°C/gas 7. Butter a 1.5 litre ovenproof dish. Chop the potatoes into even chunks, then put in a pan of lightly salted cold water and bring to the boil. Cook for 10 minutes or until just tender.
2. Slice the onions very thinly and chop the tarragon in the meantime. Put the tarragon, taters, and onions in the ovenproof dish. Crush the garlic, then combine it with the potatoes, double cream, and fino sherry. Season.
3. Grate 50g gruyère or vegetarian alternative and sprinkle over the top, along with the breadcrumbs. Bake in the oven for 25 minutes or until the top is golden and crisp.

Nutritional Value Per Serving :

Calories: 260	fat: 7.8g
protein: 7g	carbs: 36.2g
Fibre : 3.7g	Sodium:0.3g

Steamed veg with sautéed onion, garlic, lemon and tarragon dressing

Prep time: 15-20 min + simmering time 20 min
Cook time: 35 min
Serves 6

Ingredients

- A glug of olive oil
- 1 finely chopped onion
- 1 crushed garlic clove
- Finely grated zest and juice of 1 lemon
- A bunch of roughly chopped fresh tarragon

- 5 tbsp extra-virgin olive oil
- 500g sliced leeks
- 1 broccoli, separated into florets (slice thick stems)
- 200g frozen peas

Preparation Instructions :

1. Set a large pan with half full of water on the stove to boil. Make the dressing in the meantime. Put a generous amount of olive oil in a medium frying pan over medium heat. After 10 minutes of frying with the chopped onion added, stir in the crushed garlic. Cook for a further 2 to 3 minutes, then transfer to a large serving bowl and combine with lemon zest and juice, tarragon that has been finely chopped, and extra virgin olive oil. according to taste.
2. When the water is just boiling, put a colander or steamer over it (not touching the water). Add the leeks, broccoli and frozen peas. Cover and steam for 3-4 minutes until just cooked but still crunchy (you may need to do this in batches). Tip the steamed veg into the bowl that contains the dressing, then toss well and serve.

Nutritional Value Per Serving :

Calories: 215	fat: 14g
protein: 7.2g	carbs: 10.9g
Fibre : 8.2g	Sodium:0g

Cauliflower wellington

Prep time: 45 min
Cook time: 35-40 + cooling and chiling
Serves 6

Ingredients

- 1 large cauliflower, leaves removed and stem trimmed flat at the base
- Olive oil for drizzling
- 500g block ready-made all butter puff pastry
- 150g mature cheddar
- 1 free-range egg, beaten, to glaze

- For the mushroom pâté
- Olive oil for frying
- 20g butter
- 1 onion, finely chopped
- 2 garlic cloves, crushed
- 250g chestnut mushrooms, chopped
- A few fresh rosemary and thyme sprigs, leaves chopped
- 100ml dry sherry
- 100g full-fat cream cheese
- Small bunch fresh flatleaf parsley, chopped
- Squeeze lemon juice to taste
- For the gravy
- 2 tbsp rapeseed oil
- 1½ tbsp plain flour
- 200ml red wine
- 30g dried wild mushrooms, soaked in 300ml boiling water
- 1 tsp soy sauce
- 1 tbsp balsamic vinegar
- 1 tsp sugar

Preparation Instructions :

1. The oven should be heated to 200°C/180°C fan/gas 6. Place the cauliflower in a roasting pan, add a little oil, and salt and pepper to taste. 30 minutes of roasting should be enough to make the food soft and golden.

2. Meanwhile make the mushroom pâté. Heat a glug of oil and the butter in a large deep frying pan, then add the onion and fry over a medium heat for 5 minutes until soft. Add the garlic, mushrooms, rosemary and thyme and fry for 10 minutes more.

3. Add the garlic, thyme sprigs, and pearl barley, then fry for a few minutes. Turn up the heat, add the wine, and bubble to reduce for 5 minutes, then add the stock and simmer for 20-25 minutes until the barley is nearly tender, stirring occasionally with a wooden spoon. Stir in the cream, the reserved cauliflower leaves,

and the lemon juice, then simmer for another 5 minutes.

4. Roasted cauliflower should be removed from the oven and left to cool completely. Spread the mushroom pâté evenly over the surface once it has cooled.

5. Roll out the pastry until 0.5cm thick and large enough to encase the cauliflower. Grate half the cheddar over the pastry, then sit the cauliflower, florets-side down, in the centre. Bring the pastry up over the cauliflower and fold the edges over the base of the cauliflower, sealing as you go and making sure there are no gaps.

6. Line a baking sheet with non-stick baking paper. Put the cauliflower on the tray, then brush all over with half the beaten egg. Chill for 30 minutes, then brush with the remaining egg. Bake for 25 minutes until the pastry is golden and almost cooked through, then top with the remaining cheese. Bake for a further 10-15 minutes until golden and oozing.

7. Meanwhile, make the gravy. Put the oil and flour in a large saucepan and stir well, bring to a simmer over a medium heat, then cook, stirring, for 2-3 minutes. Whisk in the wine using a balloon whisk. Add the soaked mushrooms and their liquid, then simmer for 10-15 minutes. Taste and season, then add the remaining ingredients and a little water, if needed, to bring it to your preferred consistency. Serve wedges of the cauliflower wellington with the gravy and steamed vegetables, if you like.

Nutritional Value Per Serving :

Calories: 705   fat: 46.4g
protein: 18g carbs: 39.7g
Fibre : 6.7g Sodium:1.5g

Butter bean and vegetable stew

Prep time: 40 min
Serves 4

Ingredients

- Large glug of olive oil
- 2 sliced red onions
- 1 sliced leek
- 2 sliced red peppers
- 2 finely sliced carrots
- 150ml dry white wine
- 2 tbsp tomato purée
- few fresh rosemary sprigs
- 2 x 400g tins of chopped tomatoes
- 400g tin of drained butter beans
- 400g tin of drained red kidney beans
- 200g baby leaf spinach
- 1½ tbsp garam masala
- Handful of chopped fresh parsley
- To serve
- Natural yoghourt
- Extra chopped fresh parsley

Preparation Instructions :

1. Heat the oil in a deep casserole over a medium heat, add the onions, leeks, peppers, and carrots, then fry for 5-8 minutes until softening.
2. Stir in the wine, tomato purée and a few fresh rosemary sprigs and bubble for 2 minutes. Add the chopped tomatoes, season, and simmer for 15 minutes, then stir in a the butter beans and a red kidney beans and cook for 10 minutes more.
3. Stir in the spinach, garam masala, and a handful of chopped fresh parsley, then serve with natural yoghourt and extra chopped fresh parsley.

Nutritional Value Per Serving :

Calories: 365	fat: 8.3g
protein: 15.5g	carbs: 40.9g
Fibre : 18.9g	Sodium:0.3g

Veggie cottage pie stuffed jackets

Prep time: 25 min
Cook Time : 50-55 min
Serves 6

Ingredients

- 1 celeriac, trimmed and cut into 1cm wedges
- 6 medium shallots, peeled and halved lengthways
- 250g portobellini mushrooms, halved or quartered if large
- A few fresh thyme sprigs
- 4 tbsp olive oil
- Large handful kale, thickly sliced
- 2 fresh rosemary sprigs
- Small handful fresh sage leaves
- Pinch sea salt flakes
- Quality veggie gravy to serve
- For the batter
- 225g plain flour
- Pinch baking powder
- 4 large free-range eggs
- 300ml whole milk
- 3 tbsp creamed horseradish
- 2 fresh thyme sprigs, leaves picked

You'll also need...

- 1500ml baking dish or shallow casserole

Preparation Instructions :

1. The oven should be heated to 200°C/180°C fan/gas 6. In a large roasting pan, combine the celeriac, shallots, mushrooms, and the most of the thyme sprigs. Drizzle with 2 tablespoons of the oil, and season with salt and pepper. Roast the vegetables for 25 minutes, turning them halfway through, or until they are tender and starting to caramelize.
2. In a large, deep frying pan over medium-high heat, heat a little amount of oil. Stir in the raw mushrooms after cooking the

celery and carrot for 15 minutes with a touch of salt. Turn the heat to high and stir-fry for 6 to 8 minutes. After cooking the garlic for one minute over medium heat, add the tomato paste, sage, and walnuts. Cook for 2 to 3 minutes while stirring.

3. Drain the mushrooms, reserving the liquid, then roughly chop. Add to the pan with the flour. Cook for a few minutes, then stir in the stock. Pour in the chopped tomatoes and mushroom soaking liquid (minus the last 1-2 tbsp that might be gritty), then bring to the boil. Simmer over a low-medium heat for 30 minutes.

4. Add the lentils, tamari, and plenty of freshly ground black pepper after stirring, and cook for a further 15 minutes, or until thick and reduced. Season to taste.

5. Once the potatoes are tender, cut off the top third of each and use a spoon to scoop out the inside into a bowl. Fill each potato with the cottage pie filling. Mash the potato with a knob of butter, then dollop on top of each potato. Top with the cheese and bake for 15-20 minutes until melted and golden. Serve with buttered greens, if you like.

Nutritional Value Per Serving :

Calories: 353   fat: 15.2g
protein: 14.4g   carbs: 35.8g
Fibre : 7.8g   Sodium:2.3g

Caramelised onion risotto with ale and balsamic vinegar

Prep time: 1 hour and 15 min
Serves 4

Ingredients
- Olive oil for frying
- 3 red onions, finely sliced
- 1½ tbsp brown sugar
- 1.2 litres vegetable stock
- 2 garlic cloves, crushed
- 300g vialone nano risotto rice (from Ocado, Waitrose and delis)
- 350ml pale ale (we used Tribute Cornish pale ale)
- Juice 1 lemon
- 2½ tbsp balsamic vinegar
- 2 tbsp crème fraîche
- 200g chard, roughly chopped
- Bunch fresh parsley, leaves picked and roughly chopped
- 50g freshly grated parmesan (or vegetarian alternative) or crumbled goat's cheese to serve

Preparation Instructions :

1. Heat a glug of oil in a large, deep heavy-based frying pan over a low-medium heat. Add the onions and fry for 30 minutes until soft and beginning to caramelise. Add the sugar and cook for 5 minutes more.

2. In another pan, warm the stock. The rice will start to turn translucent at the edges after 5 minutes of cooking the garlic and rice with the onions in the pan.

3. Pour most of the ale into the pot while stirring and cooking until the liquid has been absorbed. Ladle by ladle, start adding the warm stock; wait until the liquid has been absorbed before adding more; and stir constantly until the rice is nearly cooked through (30-35 minutes).

4. Add the lemon juice, balsamic vinegar , crème fraîche, remaining ale, and chard. Cook for a further 5 minutes, adding water or more stock to loosen the risotto if it thickens too much. Stir in the parsley and serve straightaway with the grated or crumbled cheese.

Nutritional Value Per Serving :

Calories: 513   fat: 13.5g
protein: 13.3g   carbs: 79.6g
Fibre : 3.8g   Sodium:2.3g

Roasted vegetable yorkshire pudding traybake

Prep time: 25 min and 50-55 min
Serves 6

Ingredients

- 1 celeriac, trimmed and cut into 1cm wedges
- 6 medium shallots, peeled and halved lengthways
- 250g portobellini mushrooms, halved or quartered if large
- A few fresh thyme sprigs
- 4 tbsp olive oil
- Large handful kale, thickly sliced
- 2 fresh rosemary sprigs
- Small handful fresh sage leaves
- Pinch sea salt flakes
- Quality veggie gravy to serve
- For the batter
- 225g plain flour
- Pinch baking powder
- 4 large free-range eggs
- 300ml whole milk
- 3 tbsp creamed horseradish
- 2 fresh thyme sprigs, leaves picked

You'll also need…

- 1500ml baking dish or shallow casserole

Preparation Instructions :

1. Heat the oven to 200°C/180°C fan/gas 6. In a large roasting pan, combine the celeriac, shallots, mushrooms, and the most of the thyme sprigs. Drizzle with 2 tablespoons of the oil, and season with salt and pepper. Roast the vegetables for 25 minutes, turning them halfway through, or until they are tender and starting to caramelize.

2. Drizzle the remaining 2 tbsp oil into the 1.5 litre baking dish, then warm in the oven for 5 minutes.

3. Sift the flour and baking powder into a large mixing bowl before creating a well in the center to hold the batter. Add the milk after cracking the eggs. Make a smooth batter by beating with a balloon whisk (you should see bubbles start to appear on the surface). Add salt, pepper, and the horseradish after whisking in the thyme leaves.

4. Sprinkle the kale into the warm oil in the baking dish/casserole, then pour in the batter and arrange the roasted veg on top. Bake for 25-30 minutes until puffed up, golden and cooked through.

5. The remaining thyme sprigs, the leaves from the rosemary sprigs, and the sage leaves should all be chopped roughly. Blend in the salt. Pour over the pudding to serve, along with some mustard and horseradish sauce, and a jug of sizzling hot gravy.

Nutritional Value Per Serving :

Calories: 353	fat: 15.2g
protein: 14.4g	carbs: 35.8g
Fibre : 7.8g	Sodium:2.3g

Pearl barley and vegetable stew

Prep time: 20 min and 40 min Simmering time
Serves 4

Ingredients

- 1 tbsp olive oil
- 1 onion, sliced
- 250g pearl barley
- 800g mixed root vegetables, chopped into 2cm chunks (we used parsnips and butternut squash)
- 100ml dry white wine
- 1.5 litres vegetable stock
- 200g sliced kale
- Grated zest and juice 1 lemon

- 60ml crème fraîche
- Freshly grated parmesan (or vegetarian alternative) to serve – optional

Preparation Instructions :

1. Heat the olive oil in a large casserole and cook the onion over medium heat for 5 minutes, until it starts to soften. Add the barley and cook for a few minutes, then stir in the chopped vegetables and fry gently for 5 minutes.
2. Turn up the heat to high and add the white wine, reduce over the heat for a minute, then pour in the stock. Turn the heat down and simmer, uncovered, for 40 minutes on low heat.
3. When the vegetables are tender and the barley is cooked, stir in the kale and lemon zest and juice, then simmer for 5 minutes. Stir in the crème fraîche and sprinkle with the parmesan, if you like.

Nutritional Value Per Serving :

Calories: 454   fat: 11.5g
protein: 10.7g   carbs: 68.1g
Fibre : 8.7g   Sodium:2.4g

Butternut squash stuffed with pesto rice

Prep time: 20 min
Cook time : 1 hour to 15 min
Serves 4

Ingredients

- 2 small butternut squash, halved lengthways, seeds removed
- 2 garlic cloves, crushed
- 2 tsp chilli flakes, plus extra to serve
- Light olive oil for frying and rubbing
- 200g basmati and wild rice, rinsed (you can buy it ready-mixed in packets – we used Tilda)

- 30g dried wild mushrooms, soaked in 200ml boiling water for 30 minutes
- 100g feta, crumbled
- 50g pine nuts, lightly toasted
- For the pesto
- 50g chopped kale
- 1 garlic clove, crushed
- Large bunch fresh basil, roughly chopped
- Large bunch fresh parsley, roughly chopped
- 60g vegetarian parmesan-style cheese
- 80ml extra-virgin olive oil
- Grated zest and juice 1 lemon, plus extra to serve

Preparation Instructions :

1. Heat the oven to 220°C/200°C fan/gas 7. Put the halved butternut squashes on a baking sheet, cut-side up, and rub the cut sides with the crushed garlic, chili flakes, and a little olive oil. Season, then roast for 1 hour until tender.
2. Meanwhile, make the pesto. To make a rough paste, combine all the ingredients in a food processor (or two batches in a mini-chopper). (An alternative would be to finely chop the ingredients by hand and combine them in a mixing dish.)
3. Bring a pan of water to a boil and add the rice. Simmer for 12-15 minutes until just tender but still with some bite left. Drain well and transfer to a mixing bowl. Stir in the kale pesto. Strain the soaked mushrooms through a fine sieve, then add to the rice (discard any grit left behind in the sieve). season to taste.
4. Divide the pesto rice among the 4 cavities of the butternut squash halves. Sprinkle over the feta, then return the filled squash to the oven for another 10–15 minutes until the cheese has turned golden and everything is piping hot.
5. Serve sprinkled with the toasted pine nuts, chilli flakes, and a squeeze of lemon.

Nutritional Value Per Serving :

Calories: 753	fat: 40.4g
protein: 24.6g	carbs: 66.2g
Fibre : 13.2g	Sodium:1.2g

Baked sweet potatoes with spicy chickpeas

Prep time: 15 min
Cook time : 35-40 min
Serves 4

Ingredients

- 4 large sweet potatoes
- Olive oil for drizzling and frying
- 100g feta, crumbled
- 1 red onion, finely sliced
- 200g kale
- 50g harissa
- ½ bunch spring onions, thinly sliced (green tops included)
- 2 x 400g tins chickpeas, drained and rinsed

Preparation Instructions :

1. Heat the oven to 200°C/ 180°C fan/gas 6. On a baking sheet, place the sweet potatoes and sprinkle with a little oil. Bake until soft, about 35 to 40 minutes. Cut the potatoes in half and sprinkle the feta on top with 5 minutes left. Once the feta begins to turn brown, put the pan back in the oven.

2. Red onion should be fried in a little oil in a frying pan for 5 to 10 minutes, or until soft, halfway through the sweet potato cooking process (approximately 15 minutes before they are finished). Stir-fry the kale and harissa for two to three minutes after adding a little water. Add the spring onions and chickpeas and heat through, then season.

3. Spoon the chickpea mixture over the sweet potatoes and serve.

Nutritional Value Per Serving :

Calories: 607	fat: 16.7g
protein: 18.1g	carbs: 85.5g
Fibre : 19.8g	Sodium:1.2g

Butterbean and vegetable stew

Prep time: 30 min
Serves 4

Ingredients

- Olive oil for frying
- 2 onions, finely sliced
- 2 garlic cloves, crushed
- 4 carrots, chopped into 1cm cubes
- 600ml passata
- Pinch caster sugar
- 200g frozen spinach
- 2 x 400g tins butterbeans, drained and rinsed
- ½ large bunch fresh flatleaf parsley, chopped
- Handful fresh basil, roughly chopped
- To serve
- Crusty baguette slices

Preparation Instructions :

1. Heat a glug of oil in a large flameproof casserole over medium heat. Add the onions and fry for 2-3 minutes, then add the garlic and carrots. Fry for a further 5–10 minutes until the carrots start to soften.

2. Add the passata along with 200 ml of water and a pinch of sugar. Bring to a simmer and bubble for 5 minutes, then add the spinach and beans. Simmer for a further 10 minutes until hot, then taste and season with salt and pepper.

3. Stir through the parsley and basil, then serve in bowls with crusty baguette slices.

Nutritional Value Per Serving :

Calories: 273	fat: 17.4g
protein: 11.9g	carbs: 32g
Fibre : 15.2g	Sodium:0.9g

Roast potatoes and parsnips

Prep time: 10 min
Cook Time: 1 hour and 15 minutes
Serves 8

Ingredients
- 2kg large floury potatoes
- 1kg small parsnips (if large, halve lengthways)
- 1 tbsp Maldon sea salt
- 10 fresh rosemary sprigs
- 8 tbsp vegetable oil

Preparation Instructions :
1. Set the oven's temperature to 190°C/fan 170°/gas 5. Potatoes are cut in half. placed in a big pan of salty water Cook for 3 minutes after bringing it to a boil. Add the parsnips and cook for another three minutes.
2. Meanwhile, grind the salt and rosemary leaves in a pestle and mortar. Sprinkle on the veg.
3. Put the oil into the oven's tray (that slots into the rungs of the oven) and pop it in the oven for 5 minutes. Tip the vegetables into the tray, toss, and roast for 1 hour. Increase the temperature to 200C/fan180C/gas 6. Turn the vegetables, then cook for 15 minutes, until golden and crispy.

Nutritional Value Per Serving :

Calories: 368	fat: 12.9g
protein: 7.5g	carbs: 58.8g
Sodium:2.3g	

Warmed asparagus and lettuce

Prep time: 40 min
Serves 4

Ingredients
- 3 tbsp olive oil
- 2 small onions, cut into eighths and separated into petals
- 500g asparagus, woody ends snapped off, sliced 1cm thick diagonally
- 1 mushroom stock cube, dissolved in 200ml hot water (or mushroom soaking water from 10g dried mushrooms – or vegetable stock)
- 4 little gem lettuces, quartered lengthways
- 5g mint (about ¼ supermarket bunch), leaves picked, finely chopped

Preparation Instructions :
1. Heat the oil in a large, deep frying pan over medium heat. Add the onions and cook for 8–10 minutes, stirring often, until they soften. They should still hold their integrity in the final dish, so don't cook them until they collapse.
2. Add the sliced asparagus to the pan and toss well to combine. Keep stirring for 1 minute, then add the stock. Simmer for 3 minutes.
3. Once the asparagus is tender, remove it from the heat and add the lettuce, turning to coat with the cooking liquid and wilt the leaves. Season to taste. Finally, stir in the mint and serve.

Nutritional Value Per Serving :

Calories: 139	fat: 9.3g
protein: 4.7g	carbs: 6.7g
Fibre : 4.4g	Sodium:0.8g

Brussels sprouts with chestnuts

Prep time: 20 min
Cook time: 40 min Serves 8

Ingredients

- 1 pound fresh chestnuts
- 1 pound Brussels sprouts, halved
- 3 tablespoons butter
- 2 medium shallots, minced
- 1 pinch of ground nutmeg, or to taste
- salt and ground black pepper to taste

Preparation Instructions :

1. Score the flat side of each chestnut with an X. Place the chestnuts in a large pot filled with water and bring them to a boil. Cook for 10 minutes, then remove chestnuts from the pot and allow to cool slightly.
2. Peel the outer shell and brown skin off cooked chestnuts. Return the chestnuts to the pot and boil again over medium heat until tender, about 20 to 25 minutes. Drain and set aside.
3. At the same time, bring another large pot of lightly salted water to a boil. Add Brussels sprouts and cook, uncovered, until tender, 7 to 10 minutes. Drain in a colander, then immediately immerse in ice water for several minutes until cold to stop the cooking process.
4. Transfer the cold Brussels sprouts to a colander and drain well.
5. Melt butter in a skillet over medium heat. Add shallots; cook and stir until shallots have softened and turned translucent about 5 minutes. Stir in chestnuts and Brussels sprouts. Season with nutmeg, salt, and pepper. Continue to cook, stirring occasionally, until heated through, about 5 minutes.

Nutritional Value Per Serving :

Calories: 184	fat: 5g
protein: 3g	carbs: 32g
Sodium:4.8g	

Pomegranate fattoush

Prep time: 15 min

Cook time: 12-15 min

Serves 4-6

Ingredients

- 2 pitta bread
- 2 tbsp extra-virgin olive oil, plus extra to drizzle
- 1 tsp dried oregano
- 1 tbsp pomegranate molasses
- 1 lemon
- 1 garlic clove
- ½ pomegranate
- 500g ripe, mixed-color tomatoes
- 1 small or ½ large cucumber
- 6 spring onions
- 1 bunch of flatleaf parsley
- 6 radishes
- 1 cos lettuce or 2 little gem lettuces
- 1 tsp sumac

Preparation Instructions :

1. Heat the oven to 160°C fan/ gas 4. Pita bread should be spread open like a book and drizzled with olive oil, oregano, and some seasoning. Place in the oven for 12 to 15 minutes, or until crisp and gently brown. After allowing them to cool for ten minutes, cut them into pieces.
2. Make the dressing while the pitas are baking. The 2 tbsp oil, the lemon juice, the pomegranate molasses, and the mixture should be whisked or shaken together. With the flat of your knife, peel and crush the garlic clove, then add it to the dressing. Whisk all together and generously season with salt and pepper before setting aside. Pick out the seeds from the pomegranate and set them aside.
3. Roughly chop the tomatoes, then trim and chop the cucumber (if you're using a large cucumber, halve it lengthways and scoop out the middle). Trim and finely slice the spring onions. Pick the parsley leaves and finely chop them. Trim and thinly slice the radishes. Trim and roughly chop the cos or little gems. Toss everything together with the dressing (discarding the garlic) and

spread it out on a platter. Scatter over the toasted pitta and the pomegranate seeds, and sprinkle over the sumac. Serve.

Nutritional Value Per Serving :

Calories: 125	fat: 4.1g
protein: 3.3g	carbs: 17.4g
Fibre : 2.5g	Sodium:.3g

Taco slaw with pink pickled onions

Prep time: 15 min

Serves 4-6

Ingredients

- 1 red onion, finely sliced
- Juice of 5 limes
- 1 garlic clove, finely chopped
- 1 tsp cumin seeds
- ½ tsp chipotle flakes (optional)
- ½ tsp sugar
- 1/4 white cabbage, finely shredded
- 2 carrots, finely shredded
- 1 jalapeño chili, finely chopped
- A handful of coriander, finely chopped
- 1 tbsp rapeseed oil

Preparation Instructions :

1. Put the sliced red onion in a heatproof bowl, cover with boiling water for 20 seconds, then drain well and return to the bowl. Squeeze in the lime juice, then add the garlic, cumin seeds, chipotle flakes (if using), sugar, and a big pinch of salt. Stir well, then set aside for at least 20 minutes to quick-pickle.

2. While the onion pickles, put the shredded cabbage and carrot in a colander. Add the finely chopped jalapeño and a good pinch of salt, then scrunch together and set aside for 10 minutes to drain.

3. Squeeze the cabbage mixture to remove excess water, then put it in a mixing bowl. Add the pickled onions, along with the

pickling lime juice. Sprinkle in a handful of finely chopped coriander, drizzle in the rapeseed oil, and give everything a mix. Then taste and add extra salt if needed.

Nutritional Value Per Serving :

Calories: 57	fat: 2.2g
protein: 1.1g	carbs: 6.8g
Fibre : 3.1g	Sodium:0.6g

Roasted carrots with baby turnips

Prep time: 15 min

Cook time: 10 Min

Serves 6

Ingredients

- 12 baby turnips (about 45g each)
- 200g pack of mini carrots
- 2 tbsp olive oil

Preparation Instructions :

1. Preheat the oven to 220°C/fan 200°C/ gas 7. Bring a saucepan of water to a boil, add the unpeeled turnips, and cook for 12 minutes, or until tender. Drain and cover.

2. Meanwhile, put the carrots into a roasting dish. Drizzle with the oil and season with sea salt and freshly ground black pepper. Roast for 10 minutes, or until just tender.

3. Add the boiled turnips to the dish and mix with the carrots to coat in the oil. Serve alongside the beef with some cooked broccoli, if you like.

Nutritional Value Per Serving :

Calories: 65	fat: 4g
protein: 1g	carbs: 6.9g
Sodium:0.1g	

Roasted vegetables

Prep time: 15 min

Cook time: 10 Min

Serves 6

Ingredients

- 400g small carrots, trimmed
- 400g parsnips, halved and trimmed
- 650g small floury potatoes, cut into even-sized pieces
- 2 small red onions, each cut into 8 wedges
- 4 tbsp olive oil
- Splash of white wine vinegar
- Leaves from a few fresh thyme sprigs
- A handful of chopped fresh parsley

Preparation Instructions :

1. To prepare: Preheat the oven to 200°C/fan180°C/gas 6. Place each veggie in a large roasting pan. Sprinkle the vinegar and oil on top. Add a generous amount of spice and sprinkle on the herbs. Use your hands to combine. Over the vegetables, create a foil tent and securely seal it.
2. To cook: Roast for 30 minutes. Uncover and roast for a further 30 minutes, tossing occasionally.
3. To serve: Tip the vegetables onto a platter and serve.

Nutritional Value Per Serving :

Calories: 225	fat: 8.6g
protein: 4.3g	carbs: 34.6g
Sodium:0.1g	

Jersey royal potatoes and wild mushrooms

Prep time: 25 min

Serves 8

Ingredients

- 400-500g jersey royals, as wee as possible and scrubbed, not peeled
- 4 tbsp rapeseed or mustard oil (or a mild olive oil for cooking)

- 2 garlic cloves, sliced
- 1 red chili, sliced (deseeded, if you like)
- 100g wild mushrooms, cleaned and sliced if large
- Juice of 1 lime
- A bunch of fresh chives and a bunch of fresh dills, roughly chopped

Preparation Instructions :

1. Boil the potatoes in plenty of salted water for 8-12 minutes (the larger they are, the longer you should cook them), or until just tender. Drain and cool thoroughly, then slice in half lengthwise. Set aside.
2. Put the oil in a large pan or wok over high heat. When hot, add the garlic, chili, and mushrooms. Fry briskly (think stir-fry) until they start to crisp a little and catch—it will only take 2 minutes, tops. Remove with a slotted spoon and set aside.
3. Add the potatoes to the hot wok and fry just as fast for 3–4 minutes, so that they catch a tiny bit too. Take the wok off the heat and stir through the mushrooms. Add the lime juice and all the herbs. The herbs must wilt; they sweeten up slightly that way. Season to taste and serve warm, if possible.

Nutritional Value Per Serving :

Calories: 177	fat: 11.5g
protein: 2.7g	carbs: 18.6g

Courgette, fennel, and potato salad

Prep time: 20 min

Serves 4

Ingredients

- 50ml extra-virgin olive oil, rapeseed oil or sunflower o,il
- Finely grated zest and juice of 2 lemons (unwaxed, if possible)

- 6 small courgettes
- 1 fennel bulb, cored and thinly sliced, any fronds reserved to garnish
- 3 medium waxy potatoes

Preparation Instructions :

1. In a large bowl, combine the oil, lemon zest, and lemon juice with a generous pinch of sea salt to make a thin dressing. Using a wide vegetable peeler, peel the courgettes lengthways into thin strips. Add the fennel to the dressing. Fold everything together so that the dressing covers all the vegetables. (The lemon juice and salt will just 'cook' the courgette and soften it up.) Leave this mix to stand for 30 minutes, stirring halfway through.

2. Meanwhile, cut the potatoes into bite-size pieces. Boil in plenty of salted boiling water for about 8–10 minutes, or until they are just tender but in no danger of falling apart. Drain thoroughly and set aside to cool slightly.

3. Toss the warm potatoes with the courgette and fennel mixture, and season with black pepper. Divide between plates, garnish with any reserved fennel fronds and serve with plenty of really good rustic bread to mop up the dressing.

Nutritional Value Per Serving :

Calories: 277   fat: 10.2g
protein: 6.2g   carbs: 29.4g
Sodium:TRACE SALT

Cumin-roasted winter veg with lemon butter

Prep time: 20 min
Serves 4

Ingredients

- 6 small carrots
- 6 small turnips, halved if large
- 225g celeriac, cut into large chunks
- 2 red-skinned potatoes, such as Desirée, cut into large chunks
- 1 large onion, cut into wedges
- 4 tbsp olive oil
- 2 tsp cumin seeds, lightly crushed
- For the parsley and lemon butter
- 75g unsalted butter, softened
- Large handful of chopped fresh parsley
- Finely grated zest of 1 lemon, plus 2 tbsp lemon juice

Preparation Instructions :

1. Set the oven's temperature to 220°C/ fan200°C/gas 7. Place all the vegetables in a large roasting pan, cover with oil, sprinkle with cumin, and add salt and pepper to taste. Combine everything and roast for about 40 minutes, turning once, or until the vegetables are soft and starting to turn golden.

2. In the meantime, mix the butter, parsley, lemon juice, and zest. Season. Cling film it up, then chill until stiff.

3. To serve, place the roasted vegetables in a large bowl. Place the butter chunks on top of the vegetables to melt them.

Nutritional Value Per Serving :

Calories: 269   fat: 18.8g
protein: 3.8g   carbs: 23.8g
Sodium:0.2g

Rosemary and garlic roast potatoes

Prep time: 20 min
Serves 4

Ingredients

- 1.1500g small, even-size floury potatoes, such as Maris Piper
- Sunflower oil, for roasting
- 6 garlic cloves, unpeeled
- 2 large fresh rosemary sprigs

Preparation Instructions :

1. Set the oven's temperature to 200°C/ fan180°C/gas 6. Slice each potato into approximately 1 cm thick pieces after peeling. Slices of potato should be cooked for 3–4 minutes in salted water that has been brought to a boil until they are mushy on the exterior but still firm in the center. Drain well.

2. Pour a thin layer of oil into a large roasting tin – about 200ml. Place in the oven for 5 minutes to get very hot. Meanwhile, crush the unpeeled garlic cloves a little using the blade of a large knife. Remove the roasting tin, add the potatoes in a single layer, and spoon over some of the oil until they are all well-coated. Drain off the excess oil, sprinkle with the rosemary sprigs and crushed garlic cloves, and roast for 30 minutes, turning halfway through, until crisp and golden. Season lightly with salt just before serving with the roasted monkfish fillet with red wine sauce and steamed spinach with shallots.

Nutritional Value Per Serving :

Calories: 288   fat: 11.6g

protein: 5.8g   carbs: 43.1g

Sodium : 0g

Fish and chips

Prep time: 20 min
Cook time: 35-40 min
Serves 2

Ingredients

- 3 sweet potatoes, unpeeled (about 500g), sliced into thin wedges
- 400g parsnips, unpeeled, sliced into thin wedges
- Olive oil for roasting
- 50g fresh breadcrumbs
- 30g parmesan, grated
- 4 tbsp red pesto
- ½ bunch of basil leaves chopped
- 4 x 150g sustainable cod loin fillets
- 3 tbsp mayonnaise
- Steamed peas to serve (optional)

Preparation Instructions :

1. Heat the oven to 200ºC/180ºC fan/gas 6. In a large roasting pan, combine the sweet potatoes and parsnips. Drizzle with olive oil and season with salt and pepper. Roast for 35 to 40 minutes, rotating halfway through, until brown and crisp.
2. In a bowl, combine the parmesan and breadcrumbs. Combine half the red pesto and half the basil in another bowl. Place the fish on a baking sheet and spoon this mixture over it before topping it with breadcrumbs.
3. Place the fish in the oven for 15 minutes before the wedges are finished cooking. Bake until the flesh easily flakes and the top is browned.
4. Scatter the remaining basil on top of the fish. Stir the remaining pesto into the mayo and serve alongside the wedges and peas, if you like.

Nutritional Value Per Serving :

Calories: 560	fat: 23.4g
protein: 34.4g	carbs: 47.8g
Fibre : 9.2g	Sodium:1.1g

Mini Yorkshire puddings

Prep time: 20 min
Cook time: 35-40 min
Serves 12

Ingredients

- 4 tbsp sunflower oil or beef dripping
- 225g plain flour, sifted
- 4 medium free-range eggs, beaten
- 300ml milk

Preparation Instructions :

1. Preheat the oven to 200°C/fan 180°C/gas 6. Add the oil or drippings to a 12-hole patty pan and heat in the oven for 5-10 minutes until really hot.
2. Sift the flour into a bowl with a pinch of salt and black pepper. Whisk the eggs and milk together and add slowly to the flour, whisking until smooth. Divide among the holes, then bake for 12-15 minutes, until risen and golden.

Nutritional Value Per Serving :

Calories: 142
fat: 7.1g
protein: 5.1g
carbs: 15.7g
Sodium:0.1g

Chicken pot pie with a cheddar pastry

Prep time: 20 min
Cook time: 35-40 min
Serves 8

Ingredients

- 140g plain flour, plus a dusting
- ½ tsp English mustard powder
- ¼ tsp salt
- 40g unsalted butter, chilled and cut into small cubes
- 40g lard, chilled and cut into small cubes
- 80g cheddar, finely grated
- 1 free-range egg, lightly beaten
- Iced water (optional)
- Milk for brushing
- For poaching the chicken
- 1.2kg chicken, jointed – or buy chicken pieces if you prefer
- 1 carrot, cut into big chunks
- 1 celery stalk, cut into big pieces – keep any leaves
- 1 bouquet garni (1 bay leaf, some thyme sprigs, and parsley stalks, tied with kitchen string)
- 1 tsp fine salt
- For the filling
- 20g unsalted butter
- 80g unsmoked lardons or chopped bacon
- 1 small onion, finely chopped
- 1 carrot, cut into 1cm dice
- 1 celery stick, cut into 1cm dice
- 2 tbsp plain flour
- 100ml white wine
- 250ml stock (from the simmered poaching broth)
- 120g petits pois/garden peas
- 100g peeled pearl onions, frozen if you can get them
- 3 tbsp crème fraîche
- 4 tbsp chopped parsley
- 2 tbsp chopped dill (optional)

Preparation Instructions :

1. To prepare the pastry, combine the flour, salt, and mustard powder in a bowl. Once combined, rub in the butter and lard until the mixture resembles coarse crumbs but has some pea-sized fat pieces. Add the cheese and mix well. Create a well in the center and add the egg slowly while slicing the mixture with a table knife. You might not need all of the egg, and you might only need to add a small amount of ice water to bind the ingredients into a soft dough. You may make the pastry the day before; simply wrap it in plastic wrap and chill it for at least an hour.

2. In the meantime, combine the salt, carrot, celery, bouquet garni, and chicken pieces in a casserole. Just cover the chicken with water, come to a simmer, and cook over low heat for 20 to 25 minutes, or until the chicken is cooked. With tongs, remove the chicken and place it aside. To enhance the flavor of the poaching broth, simmer it for a long time—about 250 ml. Strip the meat from the chicken when it is cool enough to handle. Discard the skin and bones.

4. To make the filling, melt the butter in a large, heavy-bottomed pan over medium heat. Add the lardons and cook until crisp. Lower the temperature and add the onion, carrot, and celery, then cook gently, stirring now and then, for 5 minutes. Sprinkle with the flour and cook, stirring, for 2 minutes, then pour in the wine and reserved stock. Bring to a simmer, stirring occasionally, and cook until the sauce has thickened and is glossy. Remove from the heat, add the chicken, peas, and pearl onions, then stir in the crème fraîche, parsley, and, if you like, dill. Taste and season, then let it cool a bit.

5. Heat the oven to 180°C fan/gas 6. Roll

out the pastry between 2 sheets of baking paper dusted with flour. Spoon the filling into a 1.9-liter baking dish, brush the edges with milk, and drape over the pastry. Crimp to seal (or just press the pastry onto the edges), then make a few cuts in the top for the steam to escape. Brush with milk, then bake for 30-35 minutes until the filling bubbles through the cuts and the pastry is golden brown.

Nutritional Value Per Serving :

Calories: 570
fat: 29.8g
protein: 41.9g
carbs: 28.5g
Fibre : 4g
Sodium:1.2g

Big breakfast Yorkshire pudding

Prep time: 15 min
Cook time: 1-hour min
Serves 2-4

Ingredients

- 4 British outdoor-bred pork sausages
- Olive oil for drizzling
- 200g small tomatoes on the vine
- 2 large portobello mushrooms
- 4 British outdoor-bred streaky bacon slices
- A few sprigs of fresh thyme
- 2 fresh rosemary sprigs, halved
- 2-4 medium free-range eggs
- For the batter
- 140g plain flour
- 4 medium free-range eggs, beaten
- 200ml whole milk

Preparation Instructions :

1. To make the batter, whisk the flour and 4 beaten eggs in a bowl until smooth.

Gradually add the milk, whisking until smooth. Season with salt and pepper and set aside.

2. Heat the oven to 200°C/180°C fan/gas 6. Put the sausages in a roasting tin, drizzle over some olive oil, season, and then roast for 15 minutes to color lightly. Add the tomatoes and mushrooms to the tin, drape the bacon over the mushrooms, spoon over a little oil from the base of the tin, add the thyme and rosemary sprigs, then season again.

3. Increase the oven to 220°C/200°C fan/gas 7. Return the tin to the oven for 10 minutes, then remove it and pour in the batter. Put the tin straight back in the oven for 25-30 minutes, until the batter is puffed up and golden. Crack the remaining eggs into the low spots in the pudding, then return it to the oven for 6–8 minutes, or until the whites are set and the yolks are still runny. Serve hot.

Nutritional Value Per Serving :

Calories: 629
fat: 39g
protein: 36.6g
carbs: 31.7g
Fibre : 2.7g
Sodium:1.8g

Baked scotch eggs

Prep time: 15 min
Cook time 1-hour min
Serves 2-4

Ingredients

- 6 medium free-range eggs at room temperature
- 500g lean turkey thigh mince (2 percent fat)
- 1 tsp ground allspice
- A handful of fresh coriander leaves, finely chopped

- 2 spring onions, finely chopped
- 2 tbsp plain flour
- 2 medium free-range eggs, beaten
- 80g fresh breadcrumbs (choose wholemeal/ granary for fiber
- Olive oil cooking spray

Preparation Instructions :

1. Heat the oven to 200°C/180°C fan/gas 6. Put the eggs in a large pan of boiling water and boil for exactly 6 minutes long water and boil for exactly 6 minutes. Drain, cool under running cold water, and then shell.

2. Meanwhile, combine the turkey mince, allspice, coriander, and spring onions in a bowl, then season.

3. Divide the mince into 6 equal balls, then flatten each into a disc in the palm of your hand. Put a cooled egg in the middle, then use your other hand to mold the meat around the egg, completely enclosing it. Shape into a ball and set aside. Repeat with the remaining eggs and meat portions.

4. Put the flour, beaten eggs, and breadcrumbs in separate shallow bowls. Dust a Scotch egg with a little flour, then toss it between your hands to remove any excess. Dip into the beaten egg, shaking off any excess, then roll in the breadcrumbs. Set aside, then repeat with the other scotch eggs

5. Spray the scotch eggs all over with cooking oil. Bake on a baking sheet lined with non-stick baking paper for 20 minutes, or until lightly golden. Serve warm with mustard and salad, or cool completely and chill to eat as a cold snack

Nutritional Value Per Serving :

Calories: 304
fat: 9.7g
protein: 43.6g
carbs: 10.2g
Fibre : 0.6g
Sodium:0.5g

Steak pie

Prep time: 30 min
Cook time : 3 hour and 30 min + chilling and cooling
Serves 4

Ingredients

- 1 tranche of marrowbone, about 2cm long (optional)
- 2 tbsp plain flour
- ¼ tsp ground mace (optional)
- 800g diced braising beef (a mixture of shin and brisket is best)
- 4 level tbsp dripping, lard, or duck fat, plus extra for greasing
- 3 medium onions, roughly chopped
- 300ml stout or dark real ale
- 1 tbsp Worcestershire sauce
- 750ml-1 liter beef or chicken stock
- For the pastry
- 200g self-raising flour, plus extra for dusting
- 100g suet
- ½ tsp salt
- 1 medium free-range egg, beaten

Preparation Instructions :

1. Make the pastry first by mixing the flour, suet, and salt in a large bowl. Work the dough by hand until it is cohesive but not sticky after adding 120ml of cold water. Add 10-15ml of water if it appears dry. Wrap in plastic wrap, then chill for one hour. (The pastry can be prepared up to a day in advance).

2. If you're using a marrow flute, soak the marrowbone in cold water for 1-2 hours to remove any blood, then roast at 180°C/ fan160°C/gas 4, on a tray lined with baking paper, for 20 minutes, until slightly browned. Remove and cool completely.

3. Mace, pepper, and salt are used to season the flour (if using). Toss the flour with the meat. Heat half the fat in a wide frying

pan or casserole and, when it is starting to smoke, brown the meat in batches. Remove with a slotted spoon. Add the remaining fat to the pan with the onions and a pinch of salt and fry over low heat for 20 minutes, until the onions are soft and sweet but not brown. Add the stout or beer and the Worcestershire sauce and bring to a simmer.

4. Return the meat to the pan and cover with stock, then bring to a simmer. Lower the heat and braise, stirring occasionally, until the meat is tender – this should take 2½ hours. Top up with more stock, if it looks really dry. Once cooked, check the seasoning, then cool completely. (Again, this is perfect if made the day before assembling the pie.)

5. Grease a 1-liter pie dish and spoon in the pie filling. Plant the flute or marrowbone, cut side up, in the middle. It can sit just proud of the meat; don't push it in.

6. Preheat the oven to 240°C/fan220°C/ gas 9. Lightly flour a work surface and roll out the pastry until it is 5mm thick. Drape it over the dish, allowing it to overhang slightly. Eggwash the pastry and cook the pie for 30 minutes, covering it with foil for the last 10 minutes if it's browning too much. Serve immediately.

Nutritional Value Per Serving :

Calories: 910
fat: 56.3g
protein: 57.1g
carbs: 56.4g
Sodium:2.4g

Roast topside of beef with roasties and gravy

Prep time: 30 min
Cook time : 1½-1¾ hour

Serves 6

Ingredients

- 2 tbsp mustard powder
- 1½ tbsp sea salt
- 2 generous pinches of brown sugar
- 1 tbsp flavorless oil, such as sunflower or light olive oil
- 1.5kg British grass-fed topside of beef the roast potatoes
- 1.5kg floury potatoes (peeled weight), cut into small chunks
- 2 tbsp plain flour
- 100g beef dripping or sunflower oil
- For the gravy
- 150ml Madeira, red wine, or port, plus an extra splash
- 1-2 tbsp beef dripping
- 2 tbsp plain flour
- 500ml good quality beef stock

You'll also need
- Digital probe thermometer

Preparation Instructions :

1. Oven temperature set at 220 °C/200 °C fan/gas 8. To make a thick paste, combine the mustard powder, sea salt, brown sugar, and oil in a pestle and mortar. Put the steak in a roasting pan and rub this all over it before roasting for 20 minutes. The meat should be roasted for 50–55 minutes at 170°C/150°C fan/gas 3 12 until a digital probe thermometer inserted into the center of the meat registers 45°C for medium-rare or 55°C for medium. Remove from the oven (the joint's center temperature will briefly continue to increase) and let it rest for 20 to 30 minutes on a board. The roasting juices tin should be set aside.

2. Start the potatoes in the oven once the steak is there. They should be placed in a large pot of boiling water and simmered for 8 to 10 minutes, or until they are

soft and beginning to fall apart. Drain thoroughly and steam them in a colander for two minutes. Place the steak in the oven while heating the meat drippings/oil in a separate big roasting pan.

3. Return the potatoes to the saucepan, scatter over the flour and some salt, then shake the pan vigorously so the flour coats the potatoes and the edges roughen up.

4. Transfer the potatoes, along with any mashed leftovers that are stuck to the bottom, to the roasting tin when the fat in the tin is shimmering hot. To ensure an equal coating, turn the potatoes in the fat. On the shelf below the meat, roast.

5. When the meat is out of the oven, turn the heat up to 200°C/180°C fan/ gas 6. Toss the potatoes, then roast for another 20-30 minutes until deep golden and crisp.

6. Meanwhile, make the gravy. Put the beef roasting tin on the hob to heat, then pour in the Madeira, wine, or port. Scrape the bottom of the tin with a wooden spoon to loosen and dissolve all the sticky bits from the meat. Pour into a jug and leave to settle for a minute, then skim off the fat from the top with a spoon and put in a bowl. You should have a couple of tablespoons of fat – if not, make up the quantity with beef dripping.

7. Set a medium pan over medium heat, add the scooped fat, and then stir in the flour to make a thick paste. Cook, stirring, for 2 minutes or until the flour starts to smell biscuity. Pour in the Madeira juices, turn up the heat, and bubble until it thickens into a paste. Over a hh heat, slowly add the beef stock, stirring all the time, until you have a thick, glossy gravy. Stir through any resting juices from the meat, add an extra splash of Madeira, then taste and season. Keep warm over heat.

8. Thinly slice the meat. Serve with potatoes and gravy, with greens on the side, if you like.

Nutritional Value Per Serving :

Calories: 740
fat: 29.2g
protein: 65.7g
carbs: 50g
Fibre : 4.7
Sodium:3.9g

Toad in the hole

Prep time: 20 min
Cook time: 25 min
Serves 4-6

Ingredients

- 2 x 400g packs of British free-range pork sausages
- 2 onions, sliced into wedges
- Few fresh thyme sprigs
- 1 tbsp olive oil
- 150g polenta
- 1 tsp caster sugar
- ½ tsp bicarbonate of soda
- 170g plain flour
- 1½ tsp baking powder
- 284ml buttermilk
- 1 large free-range egg
- 25g unsalted butter

Preparation Instructions :

1. Heat the oven to 220°C/200°C fan/gas 7. Put the sausages and onions in a 23cm ovenproof frying pan. Season and add a few fresh thyme sprigs and 1 tbsp olive oil. Bake for 10 minutes.

2. Mix the polenta, caster sugar, bicarbonate of soda, plain flour, and baking powder in a mixing bowl. Add the buttermilk and egg and, using a wooden spoon, beat until smooth.

3. Remove the sausages and onions from the pan and melt the unsalted butter in it. Add

most of the polenta mix, then top with the sausages and onions, browned-side down. Spoon over the rest of the mix and bake for 20-25 minutes. Serve on its own, scattered with fresh thyme, or with a fresh tomato pasta sauce.

Nutritional Value Per Serving :

Calories: 631
fat: 35.8g
protein: 27.1g
carbs: 48.6g
Fibre : 3.3
Sodium:2.3g

Rack of venison with haggis crust and rosemary jus

Prep time: 30 min
Cook time: 30-40 min
Serves 6

Ingredients

- 15g (small handful) breadcrumbs
- 150g haggis, skin removed (the food team like MacSween)
- 1 tbsp fresh parsley, chopped
- Venison rack (7 chops), French trimmed, chine bone removed: ask your butcher to do this or buy ready-trimmed
- 2 tbsp olive oil, plus extra to drizzle
- 1-2 tbsp dijon mustard
- 30g salted butter
- 6 carrots, halved lengthways
- 6 banana shallots, halved lengthways
- 4 garlic cloves
- 3-4 fresh thyme sprigs
- For the rosemary jus
- 500ml good quality fresh or homemade beef stock
- 150ml tawny port
- 3 fresh rosemary sprigs

- 1 tbsp sherry vinegar

Preparation Instructions :

1. Set the oven's temperature to 220°C/ fan200°C/gas 7. In a food processor, pulse the haggis and breadcrumbs until the mixture is a smooth coarse meal. Add the parsley after seasoning well with salt and pepper. Repeat the last few strokes to combine, then remove to a bowl. Thinly slice the meat, or crumble everything with your hands. Serve with the potatoes and gravy, and if desired, some greens on the side.

2. After applying the 2 tablespoons of olive oil, season the venison with salt and pepper.   Heat a large, heavy-based frying pan over high heat. Add the venison when it's hot and sear for two to three minutes on each side. After removing the meat from the pan, cover it with mustard and a thin layer of haggis crust. Keep it loose, but not too loose, to prevent it from becoming claggy. Over the top, add a little olive oil.

3. Melt the butter in a frying pan over medium heat. Then, simmer gently for 5–10 minutes, stirring occasionally, until the carrots begin to take on a little color. Add the shallots, garlic, and thyme. Put in a roasting tray and sit the venison rack on top.

4. Roast for 30-40 minutes for rare to medium-rare (a digital probe thermometer pushed into the thickest part of the meat should read 50-55°C). Rest the meat in a warm place for 10-15 minutes.

5. While it's roasting, make the jus. Put the stock, port, and rosemary into a medium pan. Heat to a simmer, then reduces for 30-40 minutes until syrupy and full of flavor. Add the sherry vinegar and season to taste. Keep warm until ready to serve the venison.

6. To serve, bring the venison rack to the table and carve. One thick chop is enough per person.

Nutritional Value Per Serving :

Calories: 410
fat: 15.4g
protein: 41.6g
carbs: 20.2g
Fibre : 4.5
Sodium:0.8g

Bangers and mash with mustard gravy and apple wedges

Prep time: 50 min
Serves 4

Ingredients

- 1tbsp vegetable oil
- 8 pork and herb sausages
- 700g floury potatoes
- 2 Coxs apples
- 1 red onion, sliced
- 2tsp flour
- 150ml red wine
- 1tsp wholegrain mustard
- 1tbsp Worcestershire sauce
- 50g butter
- 50ml milk

Preparation Instructions :

1. Heat the oil in a large frying pan over high heat and add the sausages. Cook for 15 minutes, turning until brown all over.
2. Meanwhile, cut the potatoes into even chunks and put them in a large pan of cold, salted water. Bring to a boil and simmer for 15 minutes, or until tender.
3. Core the apples and cut them into wedges. Push the sausages to the edge of the pan and add the apple wedges. Cook for about 2 minutes on each side, until golden brown. Remove the apple with a slotted spoon and drain it on kitchen paper. Add the onion to the pan and cook, stirring occasionally, for 6-8 minutes, until softened. Stir in the flour and cook for 1 minute, then gradually add the wine, mustard, and Worcestershire sauce. Pour in 120 mL of hot water and allow it to bubble for a few minutes to thicken the gravy. Return the apple to the pan and season.
4. Drain the potatoes, then put them back in the same pan and return them to the heat for about 30 seconds to drive off any excess moisture. Mash well with the butter, milk, and seasoning.
5. Divide the mash between 4 plates and top with the bangers. Spoon over the mustard gravy and apple wedges. Serve with green beans.

Nutritional Value Per Serving :

Calories: 744
fat: 50.6g
protein: 17.2g
carbs: 51.8g
Sodium:2.6g

Chimichurri beef casserole

Prep time: 20 min
Cook time : 3½ Hours
Serves 6-8

Ingredients

- 4 tbsp sunflower oil
- 1.5kg chuck steak, cut into 2.5cm chunks
- 1 large onion, chopped
- 2 sweet peppers, sliced (red or yellow)
- 5 garlic cloves, sliced
- 1 large dried ancho chili or ½ tsp chipotle

chili paste

- 2 jalapeño chilies, deseeded and finely chopped
- 1 tbsp toasted cumin seeds, ground in a spice grinder or pestle and mortar
- 1 tbsp ground sweet paprika
- 400g can of chopped tomatoes
- 350ml fruity red wine (we used Argentine malbec)
- 450ml beef stock (use a stock pot if you like)
- 2 tbsp agave syrup or light muscovado sugar
- 2 tsp dried oregano
- 3 bay leaves
- Rice and/or tortillas to serve
- For the chimichurri sauce
- Large handful ul fresh mint leaves
- A handful of fresh oregano leaves
- 1-2 red chilies, seeds removed or left in, according to taste
- 2 tbsp red wine vinegar
- 1 tsp caster sugar
- 2 garlic cloves, roughly chopped
- 125ml extra-virgin olive oil
- Useful to have
- Food processor

Preparation Instructions :

1. Heat the oven to 150°C/130°C fan/gas 2. Heat 3 tbsp of the oil in a large hob-safe casserole or non-stick pan. Over a high fire, brown the meat in batches until it is evenly colored. Lift out and place on a platter for later.

2. After adding the onion and peppers, add the remaining oil. For 8 to 10 minutes, cook gently while stirring until softened. Garlic, dried and/or chili paste, jalapenos, cumin, and paprika should all be added. Fry for one minute at medium heat.

3. Add the diced tomatoes, wine, stock, syrup, dried oregano, and bay leaves to

the pan with the meat and any remaining liquids. Season lightly, cover, and then transfer to the oven for 3½ hours until the beef is meltingly tender.

4. For the chimichurri, whizz all the ingredients except the oil in a food processor with plenty of seasoning until roughly chopped (or chop as finely as you can by hand – it doesn't matter if it's chunky). Add the oil and stir to combine, or whiz again until everything is finely chopped. Taste and adjust the seasoning.

5. Serve the stew with the chimichurri drizzled over, with rice, tortillas, or both, as you prefer.

Nutritional Value Per Serving :

Calories: 485

fat: 25.4g

protein: 43.6g

carbs: 10.5g

Fibre: 3.4g

Sodium:0.5g

Balti pie

Prep time: 15 min

Cook time: 1 Hour

Serves 4

Ingredients

- 1 tbsp olive oil
- 500g beef mince
- 1 large onion, roughly chopped
- 2 green peppers, roughly chopped
- 2 medium carrots, roughly chopped
- 1kg sweet potatoes, roughly chopped
- 150ml soured cream
- Generous grating of whole nutmeg
- ½ x 283g jar balti paste (we like Patak's)
- 410g can chickpeas, drained
- 100g sultanas
- A handful of fresh coriander, chopped

Preparation Instructions :

1. Heat the oil in a large non-stick saucepan, add the mince, onion, peppers, and carrots and cook over medium heat for 15 minutes, stirring frequently, until just golden brown.

2. Meanwhile, boil the sweet potatoes in a pan of salted water for 10-15 minutes, until they are tender. Drain, then mash with the soured cream and grated nutmeg. Season well.

3. Preheat the oven to 200°c/fan180°c/gas 6. Stir the balti paste and 400 mL water into the mince mix, add the chickpeas, sultanas, and coriander, and simmer for 10 minutes.

4. Place in an ovenproof dish, top with the mash, and bake in the oven for 30-35 minutes, until piping hot.

Nutritional Value Per Serving :

Calories: 827
fat: 31. 6g
protein: 35.3g
carbs: 96.6g
Sodium:2g

Marmalade and coconut Bakewell tart

Prep time: 50 min
Cook time: 45 min
Serves 2-4

Ingredients

- For the pastry
- 150g plain flour, plus extra to dust
- 45g icing sugar
- 85g lightly salted butter, chilled, cubed, plus extra to grease
- Finely grated zest ó small orange
- 1 medium free-range egg yolk
- 2 tsp orange juice
- For the filling
- 125g lightly salted butter, softened
- 125g caster sugar
- 2 medium free-range eggs
- 25g plain flour
- 125g ground almonds
- 25g desiccated coconut
- 1 tsp orange flower water (from supermarkets, also sold as orange blossom water)
- 6 tbsp thick-cut marmalade
- To decorate
- 15g coconut flakes, toasted in a dry pan until golden
- Icing sugar for dusting

Preparation Instructions :

1. For the pastry, sift the flour, a pinch of salt, and the icing sugar into a food processor. Add the butter and orange zest, then whizz briefly until it looks like fine breadcrumbs. Beat the egg yolk with the orange juice, then add to the food processor and pulse briefly until the mix starts to clump together. (If you don't have a food processor, you can do this by hand in a mixing bowl, rubbing in the butter with your fingertips, then mixing in the liquid with a wooden spoon.) Turn out onto a lightly floured surface and knead briefly until smooth. If the pastry is very soft, chill it for15 minutes first. Roll it out until 3mm thick and use it to line a buttered 12cm x 35cm metal tin. Prick the base all over with a fork and chill for 20 minutes.

2. Heat the oven with a baking sheet inside to 200°C/fan180°C/gas 6. Line the tart case with crumpled baking paper and fill it with baking beans or rice. Bake for 15 minutes. Remove the paper and beans/rice, then bake for 3 minutes more or until crisp and light brown. Remove and set aside.

3. Turn down the oven temperature to 180°C/ fan160°C/gas 4. For the filling, use an electric hand mixer to beat the butter and sugar together in a bowl until light and fluffy.

Beat in the eggs one at a time, adding 1 tbsp flour with the second egg. Using a metal spoon, gently fold in the ground almonds, desiccated coconut, the remaining flour, and the orange flower water.

4. Spoon the marmalade over the pastry base, then top it with the filling and gently spread it to the edges. Bake for 30 minutes, or until puffed up and golden, and a skewer pushed into the center comes out clean.

5. Remove the tart from the oven and leave it to cool for 10 minutes to serve warm, or leave it on a wire rack to go cold. Scatter with the toasted coconut, dust with icing sugar, and cut into slices to serve.

Nutritional Value Per Serving :

Calories: 534
fat: 35.8g
protein: 8g
carbs: 46.3g
Fibre : 1.7g
Sodium:0.2g

Easy cottage pie

Prep time: 20 min
Cook time : 30 min + simmering 30 min
Serves 4

Ingredients

- 1 finely chopped onion
- 3 diced carrots
- 2 crushed garlic cloves
- 500g minced beef
- 150ml red wine
- 3 tbsp Worcestershire sauce
- 400g tin chopped tomatoes
- 1½ tbsp tomato purée
- a large handful of torn fresh basil leaves
- a pinch of sugar
- 100ml water
- 800g mashed potato

- 50g grated mature cheddar

Preparation Instructions :

1. Heat a glug of olive oil in a large frying pan, then add the chopped onion and diced carrots. Fry for 5-8 minutes until softening. Add the crushed garlic and minced beef, breaking up the beef with a wooden spoon. Fry for 5 minutes or until most of the mince has turned brown.

2. Worcestershire sauce, tomato purée, fresh basil, sugar, and 100 ml of water are added after the red wine, chopped tomatoes, and tomato purée have boiled for two to three minutes. 30 minutes of gentle simmering. Heat the oven to 200°C/180°C fan/gas 6.

3. Pour the beef into the 1.5-liter ovenproof dish. Top with the mashed potatoes, then sprinkle with grated cheddar. Bake for 30 minutes or until golden brown on top.

Nutritional Value Per Serving :

Calories: 708
fat: 38.5g
protein: 34.1g
carbs: 45.6g
Fibre : 7.2g
Sodium:1.2g

Chocolate and caramel popcorn trifle

Prep time: 30 min
Cooling and chilling : 3hours
Serves 8

Ingredients

150g dark chocolate, chopped
150g Rice Krispies or cornflakes (check they're gluten-free if you need them to be)
Butter for greasing
220g caster sugar
80g sweet popcorn

300ml double cream

For the chocolate custard

300ml whole milk

100g dark chocolate, grated

3 tbsp caster sugar

2 medium free-range egg yolks

1/2 tbsp cornflour

250g mascarpone

Preparation Instructions :

1. To start, prepare the custard by steaming but not boiling the milk in a pan over medium heat. Turn off the heat and stir 100g of grated chocolate into the milk to help it melt and combine.

2. With a balloon whisk, beat the sugar and egg yolks in a medium mixing bowl. Add the cornflour, and whisk again to combine. Pour the chocolate milk in gradually, whisking to combine, then return the mixture to the pan. Cook the custard while constantly stirring over medium heat until it thickens. Turn the heat off, let the mixture cool slightly, and then stir in the mascarpone. To prevent skin from forming, place a piece of damp baking paper on top, then chill for 30 minutes.

3. Melt the 150g chocolate in a bowl set over a pan of barely simmering water (don't let the bowl touch the water), stirring until smooth. Add the Rice Krispies/cornflakes, then fold them through the chocolate to fully coat. Spread the mixture on a baking tray lined with baking paper, then chill in the fridge for 30 minutes until set hard.

4. Put half the chocolate custard in a 20cm trifle dish. Add two-thirds of the chocolate Krispies or cornflakes, then spoon the remaining custard on top and smooth the surface. Cover and chill for 2 hours so the custard sets fully.

5. To make the popcorn praline, line a baking tray with foil and lightly grease it. Put the sugar in a heavy-based frying pan over high heat. Cook, shaking the pan occasionally, for 6-7 minutes until dark caramel forms. Stir in the popcorn, remove from the heat, and pour onto the tray. Cool, then break into shards. If you like, whizz half the praline in a processor to make coarse crumbs.

6. Just before serving, whip the cream until it holds its shape, then spoon the cream onto the trifle. Top with the popcorn and any crumbs, along with the rest of the chocolate Krispies/cornflakes, and serve.

Nutritional Value Per Serving :

Calories: 780

fat: 48.8g

protein: 7.2g

carbs: 76.9g

Fibre : 1.8g

Sodium:0.4g

Plum ripple ice cream with walnuts

Prep time: 45 min
Makes: 700ml

Ingredients

- 100g walnuts
- 300ml whole milk
- 200ml double cream
- 1 vanilla pod, split open, or 2 tsp vanilla bean paste
- 4 large free-range egg yolks
- 120g caster sugar
- For the plum ripple
- 200g plums, pitted and chopped
- 80g caster sugar

You'll also need

- Ice cream maker
- Useful to have
- Probe thermometer

Preparation Instructions :

1. Oven temperature set to 160°C fan/gas 4. The walnuts should be spread out on a baking sheet and toasted for 8 minutes in the oven. Chop roughly, then put aside.

2. Add the split vanilla pod (or paste), toasted walnuts, and a dash of salt to the milk and cream in a saucepan. Put over low heat and stir occasionally to completely reheat. Egg yolks and sugar should be whisked together with a balloon whisk until they are smooth and pale in color.

3. When the milk mixture begins to simmer, remove it from the heat and slowly pour around a third of it over the yolks to temper them, whisking constantly to combine. Gradually pour in the remaining milk, still whisking, and then transfer the mixture back to the pan.

4. Put the custard over low-medium heat. Whisk regularly until the mixture thickens and coats the back of a spoon (if you have a thermometer, you're aiming for 80-85°C). Remove from the heat and leave to cool, then transfer to the fridge to chill completely. (You can sit the pan in a bowl of iced water to speed up this process.)

5. While you wait for the ice cream base to chill, put the plums and sugar in a saucepan over medium heat. Cook for 15 minutes, stirring occasionally until the fruit breaks down into a thick, syrupy jam. Pass the jam through a fine sieve set over a bowl, using the back of a spoon to push the pulp through, then set it aside.

6. Once the ice cream base is chilled, pick out and discard the vanilla pod, then churn the base mixture in an ice cream maker according to the manufacturer's instructions. Once the mixture solidifies, drizzle in a little of the plum ripple and fold it through the machine a few times to create a ripple effect. Freeze the ice cream, then serve in scoops with more ripple drizzled over.

Nutritional Value Per Serving :

Calories: 780
fat: 19.5g
protein: 4g
carbs: 22g
Fibre : 0.8g
Sodium:0.1g

Oaty maple and pecan flapjacks

Prep time: 15 min
Cook time: 25 min
Makes: 16 square

Ingredients

- 300g butter, plus extra to grease
- 150g demerara sugar
- 50g maple syrup
- 125g golden syrup
- ¼ tsp ground cinnamon
- 75g shelled pecans, toasted in a dry pan and chopped
- 300g rolled oats
- 200g jumbo oats
- For the drizzle topping
- 25g white chocolate, chopped
- 2 tbsp maple syrup
- 1 tbsp shelled pecans, toasted in a dry pan and chopped

You'll also need...

- 20cm square cake tin lined with non-stick baking paper

Preparation Instructions :

1. Heat the oven to 150°C/130°C fan/gas 2. Put all the ingredients, except the nuts and oats, in a large pan with a pinch of salt and stir until melted. Add the nuts and oats and stir well with a wooden spoon to coat. Spoon the mixture into the lined cake tin, level the top, pressing down slightly, and bake for 25 minutes.

2. Remove the tin from the oven and transfer it to a wire rack. Score with 16 squares, then leave to cool completely in the tin.

3. For the topping, ut the chocolate and maple syrup in a heatproof bowl set over a pan of barely simmering water (don't let the bowl touch the water); heat until just melted, then stir and drizzle over the flapjacks. Sprinkle with chopped pecans,

then cut into squares to serve.

Nutritional Value Per Serving :

Calories: 365
fat: 22.4g
protein: 4.6g
carbs: 34.9g
Fibre : 2.8g
Sodium:0.4g

Mini burnt cheesecakes with rhubarb and orange compote

Prep time: 20 min
Cook time : 45 min + 4 hours chilling
Makes 6

Ingredients

- 32 x 280g packs of full-fat cream cheese (we used Philadelphia)
- 110g caster sugar
- 2 large free-range eggs
- 150ml double cream
- 1½ tbsp plain flour
- For the compote
- 400g rhubarb, cut into 5cm chunks
- 2 oranges
- 2 tbsp demerara sugar

You'll also need...

- 6 x 8.5cm individual cooking rings set on a baking sheet, greased and bases and sides lined with cling film

Preparation Instructions :

1. Heat the oven to 220°C/200°C fan/gas 6. Put the rhubarb in a roasting tin with the zest and juice of 1 orange and the 2 tbsp demerara. Roast for 8 minutes, then cool. Cut the remaining orange into segments over a bowl to catch any juice. Add the segments to the juice, then add the cooled rhubarb and its syrupy juice. Chill.

2. In a large mixing bowl, beat together the cream cheese and sugar, then beat in the eggs one at a time, followed by the double cream. Finally, beat in the flour.

3. Pour the mixture into the tins, then bake for 35 minutes, or until just set.with a wobble when you touch the top.

4. Leave to cool in the tin for 5 minutes, then unmold and serve warm. Or cool completely, chill for 4 hours, and serve at room temperature. Top with the rhubarb, orange segments, and any juices to serve.

Nutritional Value Per Serving :

Calories: 505
fat: 35.8g
protein: 9.9g
carbs: 34.7g
Fibre : 2.2g
Sodium:0.8g

Limoncello and blueberry scones

Prep time: 25 min
Cook time: 12-15 min
Serves 8

Ingredients

- 225g self-raising flour, plus extra to dust
- Finely grated zest 1 lemon
- 50g unsalted butter, cubed
- 2 tbsp caster sugar
- 110ml whole milk
- 300ml extra-thick double cream
- 2 tbsp limoncello
- 2 tbsp lemon curd
- Fresh blueberries to serve

You'll also need...

- 5cm fluted or plain cutter

Preparation Instructions :

1. Set the oven's temperature to 220°C/200°C fan/gas 7. Add the butter to the flour in the mixing bowl along with the lemon zest and a generous amount of salt. Using your fingertips, rub the butter into the flour mixture until it looks like breadcrumbs.

2. Add the sugar and mix with a round-bladed table knife. Create a well in the middle and add the milk. Using the knife, combine the ingredients to form a wet, sticky dough.

3. Lightly flour the work surface, then tip out the dough and lightly knead a few times until smooth. Roll out the dough until roughly 2.5cm thick.

4. Flour the cutter well, then stamp out scones, gently re-rolling the dough, and repeating until all the dough has been used up. Transfer the scones to a baking sheet, dust lightly with flour, and bake for 12–15 minutes, until well risen and golden. Transfer the scones to a wire rack to cool.

5. Put the cream in a bowl with the limoncello, then whip to soft peaks. Gently ripple the lemon curd through the mixture. Serve the scones split in half, topped with cream and a few blueberries.

Nutritional Value Per Serving :

Calories:380
fat: 24.4g
protein: 3.8g
carbs: 29.3g
Fibre : 1.1g
Sodium:0.3g

Black Forest gâteau

Prep time: 45 min
Cook time: 30 min
Serves 12-14

Ingredients

- 175g unsalted butter, softened
- 200g golden caster sugar
- 3 medium free-range eggs

- 1 tsp vanilla paste
- 100g dark chocolate, melted
- 200g self-raising flour
- 2 tbsp cocoa powder, plus extra to dust
- ½ tsp bicarbonate of soda
- 150g soured cream
- For the buttercream icing
- 125g unsalted butter, softened
- 250g icing sugar, sifted
- 50g soured cream
- 1 tsp vanilla extract
- For the shards and filling
- 300g dark chocolate, melted
- 150ml double cream
- 2 tbsp icing sugar
- 370g jar cherries in kirsch, drained, kirsch reserved

You'll also need...

- 2 x 18cm loose-bottomed cake tins, lined with compostable baking paper liner and sides greased; compostable baking paper to make the chocolate shards

Preparation Instructions :

1. Heat the oven to 180°C/160°C fan/gas 4. With an electric mixer, beat the 175g butter with the caster sugar until pale and fluffy. Beat in the eggs, one at a time, then the vanilla, 100g melted chocolate, flour, cocoa powder, and bicarb until combined. Finally, beat in the 150g soured cream. Divide between the 2 prepared tins, level the tops, and bake for 30 minutes or until risen and springy to the touch. Cool the cakes in the tins for 5-10 minutes, then turn them out onto a wire rack to cool completely.

2. To make the chocolate shards, lay out the baking paper on a work surface, then spread thickly with 300g melted chocolate. Roll up the paper straightaway, then put it in the freezer to set.

3. Make the buttercream by beating the butter with the icing sugar in a large mixing bowl until light and fluffy (put a clean, damp tea towel over the bowl when you start mixing to stop a cloud of icing sugar from escaping). Once the mixture is fluffy, beat in the soured cream and vanilla.

4. For the filling, put the double cream in a large mixing bowl, add the icing sugar and 1-2 tbsp of the kirsch, and then whisk to soft peaks using an electric mixer.

5. Put one of the sponges on a cake stand or plate and drizzle with 2 tbsp of the kirsch from the cherry jar. Spread over the cream, then scatter with half the drained cherries. Sandwich the second sponge on top and use a palette knife to cover the top and sides of the cake with the buttercream icing.

6. Meanwhile, put the remaining kirsch in a small pan and simmer over medium heat until the liquid is reduced and thick and syrupy. Set aside to cool.

7. To decorate the cake, take the rolled chocolate paper out of the freezer and leave it at room temperature for 5 minutes. Carefully unfold and separate into long shards. Dust the cake with cocoa, then stick the shards around the side of the cake. Arrange the reserved cherries on top, then drizzle with the reduced kirsch.

Nutritional Value Per Serving :

Calories:622
fat: 36.1g
protein: 5.7g
carbs: 67.4g
Fibre : 2.3g
Sodium:0.4g

Double-layer custard and chocolate mousse

Prep time: 40 min + chilling and setting
Serves 8

Ingredients

- 200ml double cream
- 500ml whole milk
- 1 tsp vanilla extract
- 4 large free-range egg yolks (set the whites aside for the mousse)
- 2 tbsp cornflour
- 80g golden caster sugar
- For the mousse
- 120g dark chocolate, plus extra for grating
- 4 large free-range egg whites
- ¼ tsp lemon juice
- 20g golden caster sugar

Preparation Instructions :

1. For the custard, put the cream, milk, and vanilla extract in a large heavy-based pan over medium heat and warm until just steaming. In a heatproof bowl, whisk the egg yolks with the corn flour and caster sugar until smooth and pale. Slowly whisk the hot cream into the egg mixture until smooth.

2. Return the custard mixture to the pan and cook over medium heat for 2-3 minutes until it forms a thick custard, whisking all the time. Divide the custard equally among 8 small bowls or glasses. Cover, then leave to set while you prepare the mousse.

3. For the mousse, melt the chocolate in a large heatproof bowl set over a pan of boiling water (don't let the water touch the bowl), then set aside to cool slightly. In a separate, clean bowl, whisk the egg whites and lemon juice until the whites form soft peaks when the whisk is removed. Slowly add the sugar, whisking between additions, until medium peaks form.

4. Spoon a large spoonful of the egg whites into the melted chocolate, then stir in quickly until combined. Add the chocolate mixture to the remaining egg whites and fold in carefully, using a large metal spoon until smooth and fully incorporated.

5. Spoon heaped spoonfuls of the mousse on top of the custard, dividing it equally among the bowls. Finish by grating over extra dark chocolate then cover and leave in the fridge to set for 3-4 hours.

Nutritional Value Per Serving :

Calories: 343
fat: 22.7g
protein: 6.4g
carbs: 28g
Fibre : 0.5g
Sodium:0.2g

Strawberry, lemon, and elderflower meringue

Prep time: 10 min
Cook time: 2 hour and 30 min + cooling
Serves 8

Ingredients

- 400ml double cream
- Grated zest and juice 1 lemon
- 3 tbsp elderflower cordial
- 300-400g ripe strawberries, hulled and sliced
- 1 tbsp unrefined caster sugar
- A few elderflower heads, in season, to decorate (optional)
- For the meringue
- 4 medium free-range egg whites
- 200g unrefined caster sugar
- Butter to grease

You'll also need...
- Electric mixer; large baking sheet; compostable

baking paper

Preparation Instructions :

1. Heat the oven to 120°C/100°C fan/gas 1. To make the meringue, put the egg whites in a large, clean bowl and whisk with an electric mixer until they form soft peaks (when you lift the beaters out, the peaks flop over). With the mixer running, add large spoonfuls of the sugar, one at a time, beating between each addition, until all the 200g sugar is incorporated. Whisk for a further 6-8 minutes until thick, pale, smooth, and glossy.

2. Lightly grease a sheet of baking paper and lay it on the baking sheet. Spoon the meringue onto the paper to form a large disc about 25cm wide with slightly peaked edges – it doesn't have to be perfect. Bake the meringue for 25-30 minutes, then reduce the heat to 110°C/90°C fan/gas ½ and bake for 2 hours more until the meringue has formed a crisp shell. Remove from the oven and allow to cool.

3. When ready to serve, pour the cream into a large bowl. Add half the lemon zest and juice and 2 tbsp of the cordial. Whisk until the cream is thick enough to hold soft peaks.

4. Put the strawberries in a bowl with the remaining lemon juice and cordial. Gently turn them to coat. Spoon the cream onto the meringue, top with the strawberries, and sprinkle with the sugar, the remaining lemon zest, and some elderflower blossoms, if you like.

Nutritional Value Per Serving :

Calories: 386
fat: 27g
protein: 2.8g
carbs: 34g
Fibre : 1.4g
Sodium:0.1g

Strawberry sundae with shortbread biscuits

Prep time: 25 min
Cook time: 25-30 min + cooling
Freezing 6 hours
Serves 6

Ingredients

For the ice cream
397g tin condensed milk
600ml double cream
1 tsp vanilla bean paste or vanilla extract
For the shortbread
200g plain flour
150g butter, cubed
75g caster sugar
For the strawberry cassis sauce
250g strawberries, hulled (150g chopped, 100g quartered)
2 tbsp cassis

You'll also need...

Electric mixer; mini chopper or stick blender
900g loaf tin or freezer-proof container lined with cling film
20cm x 20cm square cake tin, greased and lined with compostable baking paper

Preparation Instructions :

1. Put the condensed milk, cream, and vanilla in a mixing bowl, then use an electric mixer to beat until thick. Scrape into the loaf tin/container, cover, and freeze for 6 hours or overnight.

2. Next, make the shortbread. Heat the oven to 160°C/140°C fan/gas 3. Put the flour and butter in a mixing bowl, then rub together with your fingertips until the mixture resembles breadcrumbs. Stir in the sugar, then mix until it comes together. Tip into the cake tin, lightly press down with the back of a spoon to level and then bake for 25-30 minutes until pale and sandy to

the touch. Score into 8 fingers, then cool in the tin.

3. For the sauce, whizz the 150g chopped strawberries in a mini food processor (or use a stick blender) with the cassis until smooth. If you don't want seeds, push the purée through a sieve with the back of a spoon.

4. To assemble, drizzle 1 tsp sauce into 6 sundae/wine glasses, crumble in some shortbread, top with ice cream and quartered strawberries, then repeat, drizzling the remaining sauce on top.

Nutritional Value Per Serving :

Calories: 554
fat: 44.4g
protein: 4.9g
carbs: 33g
Fibre : 0.3g
Sodium:0.2g

Blueberry gin and tonic cheesecake

Prep time: 30 min
Cook time: 30 min
Cooling 8 hours
Serves 10-12

Ingredients

- 90g unsalted butter, softened, plus extra to grease
- 90g plain flour
- 45g caster sugar
- 45g semolina
- For the filling
- 200g white chocolate, chopped, plus extra to serve
- 500g full-fat cream cheese, at room temperature (180g mascarpone, at room temperature
- 250ml double cream, chilled
- 70g Scottish heather honey

- For the blueberry gin and tonic jelly topping
- 300g blueberries
- 4 gelatine leaves
- 125g caster sugar
- 200ml water
- 1 pared strip of lemon zest
- 125ml gin
- 150ml tonic water
- Pared lemon zest curls (to decorate)

You'll also need

- 20cm springform or loose-bottomed cake tin, greased and the base lined

Preparation Instructions :

1. Use a food processor to blend all the ingredients for the shortbread base with a pinch of salt until the mixture forms a soft dough. To create an even layer, press the mixture into the prepared tin. Chill for 20 minutes. Bake the foundation for 30 minutes, or until lightly golden, after preheating the oven to 160°C fan/gas 4. Set aside to cool completely.

2. Melt the white chocolate for the filling in a heatproof bowl over a pan of barely simmering water. After melting, remove from heat and let cool for a few minutes. In the meantime, whisk the cream cheese and mascarpone together in a large bowl until thoroughly combined. Once more beating is complete, add the chocolate that has been cooled.

3. In another bowl, whip the cream and honey to soft peaks (that flop over when you lift out the whisk). Gently fold the honey cream into the chocolate mix, then spoon it evenly over the base and level the top. Cover and chill for 3 hours, until firm.

4. Once the cheesecake is firm, neatly arrange the blueberries on top. Soak the gelatine leaves in cold water for 5 minutes. Combine the caster sugar, water, and a

pared strip of lemon zest in a small pan. Stir over medium heat until the sugar dissolves, then simmer for 5 minutes until syrupy. Set aside to cool slightly, then discard the zest. Squeeze the gelatine leaves to remove excess water, then stir them into the hot syrup. Stir in the gin and tonic water. Cool completely, then pour over the cheesecake and chill for at least 4 hours until set. Decorate with peeled lemon zest curls.

Nutritional Value Per Serving :

Calories: 554
fat: 44.4g
protein: 4.9g
carbs: 33g
Fibre : 0.3g
Sodium:0.2g

Fruit scones

Prep time: 15 min
Cook time: 25 min
Cooling: 8 hours
Serves 8-10

Ingredients

- 350g self-raising flour, plus extra for dusting
- 90g cold unsalted butter, cut into small pieces
- ½ tbsp baking powder
- 2 tbsp golden caster sugar
- 100g sultanas or raisins
- 150ml buttermilk
- Splash milk or double cream for glazing
- Specialist kit
- 8cm pastry cutter

Preparation Instructions :

1. Heat the oven to 180°C fan/gas 6 and put a baking sheet inside to heat up. In a large bowl, rub together the flour, butter, baking powder, and a pinch of salt until the mixture resembles breadcrumbs. Stir in the sugar and dried fruit, then quickly add the buttermilk,

mixing with a butter knife until the mixture comes together into a rough dough.

2. Tip out onto a lightly floured surface, then lightly knead 2-3 times to bring everything together (don't overwork the dough or the scones will be tough).

3. Pat the dough to an even thickness of about 3cm. Cut using a lightly floured 8cm cutter, reshaping the offcuts as needed. Carefully remove the hot baking sheet from the oven and lightly dust it with flour. Transfer the scones to the hot tray and brush the tops with a little milk or cream. Bake for 15-20 minutes, until risen and golden. Cool on a wire rack before serving.

Nutritional Value Per Serving :

Calories: 234
fat: 8.1g
protein: 4.3g
carbs: 37.2g
Fibre : 1.7g
Sodium:0.5g

Boozy raspberry Eton mess

Prep time: 20 min
Serves 6-8

Ingredients

- 500g raspberries
- 100ml crème de cassis (we love White Heron British Cassis)
- 70g icing sugar, plus 2 tbsp for the coulis
- 800ml double cream
- 1 tbsp vanilla bean paste
- 75g meringue nests, plus extra, crumbled, to serve

Preparation Instructions :

1. Put 250g of the raspberries in a blender/ food processor with the crème de cassis and the 2 tbsp icing sugar. Whizz until smooth, then push the mixture through a sieve with the back of a wooden spoon,

directly into a bowl to make a coulis (discard the pulp and seeds).

2. In a large bowl, use an electric mixer to beat the cream, vanilla paste and remaining 70g icing sugar until pillowy with a thick, droppable consistency (scoop some up on a wooden spoon, hold the spoon sideways, and tap it on the edge of the bowl – the cream should drop off reluctantly). Pour in the coulis and break in the meringue nests, keeping some nice chunky pieces. Add the remaining raspberries, then gently fold everything together with a large metal spoon, just until the coulis is rippled through the cream.

3. Portion into 6-8 glasses or small bowls, then serve topped with extra crumbled meringue if you like.

Nutritional Value Per Serving :

Calories: 646
fat: 53.9g
protein: 2.9g
carbs: 29.5g
Fibre : 2.1g
Sodium:0.1g

Plum upside-down cake

Prep time: 20 min
Cook time: 45 min
Serves 8

Ingredients

- 125g unsalted butter, at room temperature, plus extra to grease
- 250g caster sugar
- 50g runny honey
- 6 thyme sprigs
- 1 tsp salt
- 8 plums, halved and pitted
- 2 medium free-range eggs
- 100g plain flour
- 1 tsp baking powder
- 75g toasted hazelnuts, whizzed into a powder
- Crème fraîche to serve

You'll also need
- 23cm cake tin

Preparation Instructions :

1. Oven temperature set at 180°C fan/gas 6. Butter the cake pan and use baking paper to line the bottom and sides. Swirl the pan rather than stirring while you heat 150g of the sugar in it to dissolve. Add three of the thyme sprigs, the honey, and the salt once it starts to become golden. Pour into the prepared cake tin after taking the pot off the heat and letting it cool slightly. Insert the thyme sprigs in the tin's center. Place the cut-side-down plum halves in a single layer on top (chop one or two, if needed, to fill in gaps and cover the base).

2. Beat the 125g butter with the remaining sugar until pale and creamy, then add the eggs one at a time, beating the first into the mixture before adding the next. Sift together the flour and baking powder, then gently fold in with the hazelnuts using a balloon whisk. Strip the leaves off the remaining thyme sprigs and fold those through too. Pour the mix over the plums, smooth the top, then bake in the oven for 45-50 minutes until a skewer pushed into the center comes out clean.

3. Leave to cool for 5 minutes, then carefully invert the cake onto a plate. Peel away the baking paper, then cool for 5 minutes before slicing.

Nutritional Value Per Serving :

Calories: 412
fat: 20.4g
protein: 5.2g
carbs: 50.8g
Fibre : 2.3g
Sodium:0.8g

Chicken stew with lemon and herb crumb topping

Prep time: 30 min
Simmer time : 45 min
Serves 6

Ingredients

- Olive oil for frying
- 6 banana shallots, halved
- 6 skinless, boneless free-range chicken thighs, chopped
- 2 garlic cloves, crushed
- 25g butter
- 2 tbsp plain flour
- 250ml dry white wine
- 600ml chicken stock, hot
- 1 large fresh rosemary sprig, leaves removed and chopped
- 1 tbsp chopped fresh thyme leaves
- 600g chantenay carrots
- Crusty bread to serve (optional)
- For the herb crumb topping
- 50g dried breadcrumbs
- Zest ½ lemon
- Handful fresh parsley, chopped

You'll also need...
- Large casserole with a lid

Preparation Instructions :

1. Heat a glug of oil in the casserole and gently fry the shallots, covered, for 10 minutes, stirring occasionally.
2. Meanwhile, heat a glug of oil in a large frying pan over a medium heat and fry the chicken for 5-6 minutes until browned, then transfer to a plate.
3. Add the garlic and butter to the casserole and cook for a further 2 minutes. Stir in the flour and cook for 1 minute, then add the wine and bubble to evaporate most of it. Stir in the stock, bring to the boil, then add the browned chicken with the rosemary, thyme and carrots.
4. Turn the heat to low, cover and simmer for 45 minutes.
5. Meanwhile, combine all the ingredients for the herb crumb topping and season. Divide two thirds of the stew among 6 bowls, sprinkle with the topping, then serve with crusty bread, if you like.

Nutritional Value Per Serving :

Calories: 281
fat: 10.3g
protein: 19.8g
carbs: 18.4g
Fibre : 4.9g
Sodium:0.7g

Smoked haddock and jersey royal stew

Prep time: 30 min
Simmer time : 28-30 min
Serves 6

Ingredients

- 15g unsalted butter
- Good drizzle olive oil
- 4 onions, finely sliced
- 1 large garlic clove, thickly sliced
- 6 pink peppercorns
- ½ tsp coriander seeds, crushed
- ½ tsp ground turmeric
- 80g pancetta

- 300g jersey royals or other waxy potatoes such as charlotte
- 650ml good quality fish or chicken stock (preferably homemade)
- 1kg oak-smoked MSC haddock fillets, skinned and bones
- removed (where possible)
- 100g baby leaf spinach
- Crème fraîche to serve (optional)

Preparation Instructions :

1. Heat the butter and oil in a large sauté pan (use one with a lid) or flameproof casserole, then gently fry the onions for 20 minutes with the garlic, peppercorns, coriander seeds, turmeric and plenty of black pepper. Cover the pan with a lid and stir occasionally.
2. Meanwhile, slice the pancetta, quarter the potatoes and warm the fish stock. When the onions have softened and are gaining a little colour (after 8-10 minutes), add the pancetta and potatoes, then the fish stock. Bring to the boil, stir, then simmer for 20 minutes or until the potatoes feel tender when pierced with a sharp knife. Top with the smoked fish and spinach, then cover with the lid and cook for 8-10 minutes more or until the fish is lightly steamed and the spinach is wilted.
3. Evenly divide the fish and the stew among 6 shallow bowls, then top each with a spoonful of crème fraîche to serve, if you like.

Nutritional Value Per Serving :

Calories: 322
fat: 12g
protein: 42g
carbs: 9.5g
Fibre : 2.6g
Sodium:2.7g

Roasted tomato soup

Prep time: 1 hour
Serves 4

Ingredients

- 1kg ripe tomatoes, quartered
- 250g red onions, cut into thick wedges
- 4 garlic cloves
- 3 fresh rosemary sprigs
- 2 red peppers, quartered and deseeded
- 4 tbsp olive oil
- 300ml hot vegetable stock
- 1 tbsp red wine vinegar
- 2 dashes of Tabasco
- 4 dashes of Worcestershire sauce
- Few sprigs fresh parsley

Preparation Instructions :

1. Set the oven's temperature to 220°C/fan 200°C/gas 7. Place the peppers, tomatoes, onions, garlic, and rosemary in a big roasting pan. Roast for 45 minutes, until soft and starting to char. Drizzle with olive oil.
2. Two batches of the roasted veggies should be added to a food processor and blended just until combined but still rather chunky.
3. Add the stock, wine vinegar, Tabasco, and Worcestershire sauce after tipping into a big pan. Stirring and low heating. Add some freshly ground black pepper and a few parsley sprigs after dividing among the four dishes. Serve with French bread slices.

Nutritional Value Per Serving :

Calories: 203
fat: 12.4g
protein: 3.8g
carbs: 20g
Sodium:1.1g

Minted pea and watercress soup

Prep time: 45 min

Serves 4

Ingredients

- Large bunch watercress, washed, stalks and leaves separated
- 300ml vegetable stock or water
- 500ml Alpro soya dairy-free alternative to milk (unsweetened)
- 3 tbsp sunflower oil
- 1 large onion, finely chopped
- 1 medium potato, cubed
- Bunch fresh mint leaves, roughly chopped
- 400g fresh or frozen shelled peas

Preparation Instructions :

1. Chop the watercress stalks (reserving the leaves) and combine with the stock, water, and soy milk in a small pot. Bring to a simmer and cook for five minutes. Turn off the heat and let the ingredients settle.

2. Heat the oil in a large pan and add the onion. Cook on a low heat until softened but not coloured. Stir in the potato, cover the pan, and simmer until tender. With the watercress stalks removed, add the mint and peas, strain the soy milk stock into the pan, season, and boil for 2 minutes. Turn off the heat after adding the watercress leaves.

3. Set a sieve over a heatproof bowl and drain the soup through it. Put the solids caught in the sieve into a blender with a little of the soup liquid and purée. Push this mixture through the sieve into the bowl with the back of a ladle and repeat with any solids left in the sieve. Discard any bits that won't pass through. Serve warm, garnished with croutons, bacon bits and soya cream, if you like.

Nutritional Value Per Serving :

Calories: 262   fat: 12.9g

protein: 14g   carbs: 24g

Sodium:0.8g

Red beef stew

Prep time: 1 hours and 30 min

Serves 8

Ingredients

- 4 tbsp vegetable oil
- 900g lean stewing beef steak, diced
- 2 onions, chopped
- 2 tbsp paprika
- 1 garlic clove, crushed
- 1 jar tomato sauce for pasta (we like Loyd Grossman Tomato & Roasted Garlic)
- 1 tsp concentrated beef stock or ½ beef stock cube
- 2 red peppers, deseeded and cut into chunks
- 250g button mushrooms, halved
- 1 large sweet potato, cut into big chunks

Preparation Instructions :

1. In a large frying pan, heat the oil to a medium-high temperature. Beef should be fried in batches until just browned. Remove with a slotted spoon and put into a medium casserole.

2. Add the onions to the frying pan and cook for 5 minutes, stirring, until just transparent. After adding the tomato sauce and stirring in the paprika and garlic, simmer for 1 minute. Pour boiling water from the jar into the pan. The peppers, mushrooms, and sweet potato are then added after stirring in the stock cube or concentrate. Add to the casserole after bringing to a boil. Cook the meat for one hour at a medium-low simmer, or until it is tender.

3. Cool completely, then freeze in portions

for up to 3 months. Thaw for 24 hours in the fridge. To reheat, put the stew into a large pan over a medium heat and heat until piping hot or defrost and reheat in the microwave according to portion size.

4. Season to taste and serve with soured cream and jacket potatoes.

Nutritional Value Per Serving :

Calories: 284   fat: 13.4g
protein: 28.1g   carbs: 13.8g
Sodium:1.2g

Pumpkin soup with pumpkin seed pesto

Prep time: 1 hours and 30 min
Serves 8

Ingredients

- 1.25kg kabocha squash or pumpkin
- Sunflower oil
- 40g butter
- 1 medium onion, chopped
- 1.2 litres hot vegetable stock
- 4 tbsp crème fraîche
- Fresh flatleaf parsley sprigs, to garnish
- For the pumpkin seed pesto
- 30g shelled, unsalted pumpkin seeds (from supermarkets and health food shops)
- 40g fresh coriander leaves
- 1/2 green chilli, deseeded and finely chopped
- 1 fat garlic clove, crushed
- 65ml olive oil
- 25g vegetarian Parmesan, finely grated

Preparation Instructions :

1. Preheat the oven to 180°C/fan160°C/gas 4. Cut the squash or pumpkin into chunky wedges and scoop away all the fibres and seeds, leaving the skin on. Rub the squash pieces with sunflower oil and season well with salt and pepper. Put them into a small roasting tin, skin-side down. Roast for about 40 minutes or until tender. Remove the squash from the oven and transfer it onto a plate. When cool enough to handle, slice away and discard the skin, and cut the flesh into small chunks.

2. Melt the butter in a large pan, add the onion, and cook gently for about 10 minutes, until the onion is very soft but not browned. Add the roasted squash, any juices from the plate and the stock. Season, then cover and simmer for 20 minutes.

3. Meanwhile, make the pesto. Heat a dry, heavy-based frying pan over a high heat. Add the pumpkin seeds and shake them around until lightly toasted. Cool, reserving 1 tablespoon of seeds to garnish. Put the rest of the seeds into a food processor with the coriander, chilli, garlic, and oil. Blend to a paste. Transfer to a bowl and stir in the Parmesan, seasoning to taste.

4. Leave the soup to cool slightly, then liquidise in batches until smooth. Return the soup to a clean pan and bring it back to a gentle simmer. Stir in 4 tablespoons of the pesto and adjust the seasoning. Ladle into warmed bowls and garnish each with a spoonful of crème fraîche, the reserved toasted pumpkin seeds, and a sprig of flatleaf parsley.

Nutritional Value Per Serving :

Calories: 435   fat: 40.6g
protein: 8.3g   carbs: 10g
Sodium:1.4g

Vegetable stew with herb dumplings

Prep time: 1 hours
Serves 4

Ingredients

- 25g butter
- 1 onion, chopped
- 1 leek, thickly sliced and washed
- 3 carrots, roughly chopped
- 2 celery sticks, roughly chopped
- 3 tbsp plain flour
- 600ml vegetable stock or water, hot
- 410g can mixed pulses, drained and rinsed
- Few sprigs of fresh thyme
- For the herb dumplings
- 225g self-raising flour
- 110g vegetable suet
- 2 tbsp fresh thyme leaves

Preparation Instructions :

1. Melt the butter in a large saucepan over a medium heat. After adding it, sauté the onion for 5 minutes, or until tender. For an additional 10 minutes, gently tossing occasionally, simmer the leek, carrots, and celery until tender. After adding the flour, add the stock or water gradually. With the lid on, simmer the pulses after they have been drained for 20 minutes.

2. Make the dumplings in the meantime. Flour, suet, and thyme should be combined, then season to taste. To make a soft, slightly sticky dough, add around 125ml of cold water. If the dough appears a bit dry, add a little more water.

3. You should end up with 12 dumplings if you drop large spoonfuls of the dough into the simmering stew and push them in until they are just peeking out. Cover again and simmer for a further 20 minutes, until the dumplings are risen and no longer sticky. Serve with seasonal greens.

Nutritional Value Per Serving :

Calories: 642   fat: 31.5g
protein: 15.5g   carbs: 78.8g
Sodium:0.9g

Fennel soup with winter greens and bacon

Prep time: 1 hour and 30 min
Serves 4

Ingredients

- 100g butter
- 2 large leeks, sliced and washed thoroughly
- 1 tsp fennel seeds, crushed
- 3 fennel bulbs, coarsely chopped
- 900g potatoes, roughly chopped
- 1.2 litres chicken stock, hot
- 150ml whipping cream
- For the winter greens and bacon
- 1 small or ½ large savoy cabbage or other winter greens
- 50g butter
- 175g pancetta or smoked streaky bacon, diced
- Handful roughly chopped fresh thyme leaves

Preparation Instructions :

1. Melt the butter in a large saucepan over medium-low heat. Add the sliced leeks and cook gently for 10 minutes, stirring occasionally, until very soft. Add the fennel seeds and cook for 2-3 minutes. Stir in the chopped fennel and the potatoes.

2. Cover the vegetables with a sheet of wet baking paper and put a lid on the pan. Cook gently for 10-12 minutes, until the leeks are soft. Remove and discard the paper. Pour in the stock, bring to the boil, then cover and simmer for 30 minutes, until the vegetables are very tender.

3. Leave the soup to cool slightly, then pour half into a food processor or blender and whizz until smooth. Press through a sieve into the remaining soup in the pan. Stir in the cream and season to taste. Gently reheat the soup, but make sure it doesn't boil.

4. Meanwhile, make the winter greens and bacon. Discard the tough outer leaves from the cabbage. Roughly tear the remaining leaves, discarding any hard stalks, and blanch them in boiling, salted water for 2-3 minutes. Refresh under cold running water and drain.

5. Melt the butter in a large frying pan over a medium heat. Add the pancetta or bacon, and cook for 3-4 minutes, until golden. Add the cabbage and thyme, and stir-fry for about 5 minutes, until the cabbage is tender. Season well.

6. Ladle the soup into deep bowls and spoon the winter greens and bacon into each bowl to serve.

Nutritional Value Per Serving :

Calories: 808   fat: 59.4g
protein: 28.1g   carbs: 48.2g
Sodium:3.6g

Mutton, vegetable and barley stew

Prep time: 25 min
Cook time : 2-12 hours
Serves 6

Ingredients

- 1kg boned shoulder or leg of mutton, cut into 2cm dice
- 3 tbsp plain flour
- 2 tbsp olive oil
- 15g butter
- 2 celery sticks, roughly sliced
- 1 leek, washed and roughly sliced
- 2 garlic cloves, crushed
- 2 carrots, roughly sliced
- 400g floury potatoes, roughly diced
- 400g swede, roughly diced
- 500ml fresh lamb stock, hot
- 400ml carrot juice

- 2 fresh sprigs each rosemary and thyme, plus extra to garnish
- 100g pearl barley

Preparation Instructions :

1. Set the oven's temperature to 180°C/ fan160°C/gas 4. Put the flour, seasoning, and cubed mutton in a big bowl. Well, toss.

2. Place a large casserole on a high heat source. Add the oil and brown the mutton in batches.

3. Add the butter after lowering the heat to medium. Toss thoroughly after adding the celery, leek, garlic, carrots, potatoes, and swede. Cook till a light browning, stirring occasionally. Then add the rosemary and thyme after adding the lamb stock and carrot juice. Bring to a boil, cover, and simmer for 2 12 hours, or until tender, in the oven.

4. 30 minutes before the cooking time is up, stir in the pearl barley to help it absorb the liquids and become soft. The stew ought to be substantial and luscious. Serve with rustic bread and season. Garnish with rosemary and thyme.

Nutritional Value Per Serving :

Calories: 754   fat: 33.4g
protein: 61.6g   carbs: 63.1g
Sodium:1.3g

Ham hock, split pea and mint stew

Prep time: 2 hours
Serves 4

Ingredients

- 600g ham hock
- 2 carrots, roughly chopped
- 1 large onion, quartered
- 6 black peppercorns
- 150g dried yellow split peas

- 450g white potatoes, cut into cubes
- 150g frozen peas
- Small handful chopped fresh mint

Preparation Instructions :

1. In a big pan, add the ham hock, carrots, onion, and peppercorns. Add 1.7 liters of water, cover, and heat through. Reduce the heat slightly and simmer for 1 hour. Skim off any scum.

2. Strain the cooking liquid through a colander into another large pan. Pull the meat from the hock and shred it after allowing it to cool slightly. Cover and leave out. Discard the bone and the contents of the colander.

3. Bring the liquid to a simmer. Add the split peas and cook for 35 minutes, skimming off any scum. Add the potatoes and cook for 10-12 minutes or until the potatoes and split peas are tender. Stir in the frozen peas and cook for 2-3 minutes, until soft. Take off the heat and stir in most of the mint. Blend half until smooth, mix with the remainder and season.

4. Divide the stew between warmed bowls. Top with the shredded ham and reserved mint to serve.

Nutritional Value Per Serving :

Calories: 474   fat: 14.3g

protein: 40.7g   carbs: 48.6g

Sodium:3.5g

Potato, bread and garlic soup

Prep time: 40 min

Serves 4

Ingredients

- 3 tbsp olive oil
- 2 onions, finely diced
- 4 large (about 800g) floury potatoes, diced
- 600ml hot vegetable stock
- About 100g stale rustic bread, such as sourdough or ciabatta, torn into pieces
- 3-4 handfuls wild garlic, washed but whole
- Extra-virgin olive oil (preferably a peppery one), to serve
- 1 dried red chilli, crumbled, to serve (optional)

Preparation Instructions :

1. Gently heat the olive oil in a large saucepan over a medium heat. Add the onions and cook, stirring occasionally, for 5 min, until soft but not browned. Stir in the potatoes and a good pinch of sea salt, cover and reduce the heat to low. Sweat for 15-20 min or until the potatoes start to look fluffy around the edges. Check they aren't catching.ghtly and simmer for 1 hour. Skim off any scum.

2. Add the stock to the pan, increase the heat slightly and bring the soup up to a simmer but don't boil. Simmer for 6-8 min or until the potatoes are really soft. Add the bread pieces and mash them gently into the soup. You could purée the soup or, for more texture, use a potato masher.

3. Check the seasoning and thickness of the soup. Remove from the heat and add the wild garlic to wilt, or line the soup bowls with the wild garlic and then pour in the soup. Put the extra-virgin olive oil and the chilli, if using, on the table for people to help themselves. You could also garnish the soup with a grated, crumbly cheese, such as Parmesan, Pecorino or even Lancashire.th the shredded ham and reserved mint to serve.

Nutritional Value Per Serving :

Calories: 326

fat: 10.2g

protein: 8.7g

carbs: 53.4g

Sodium:0.6g

Printed in Great Britain
by Amazon

12695243R10052